Political Profiles
Sarah
Palin

Sarah Palin

Political Profiles
Sarah Palin

Lisa Petrillo

Greensboro, North Carolina

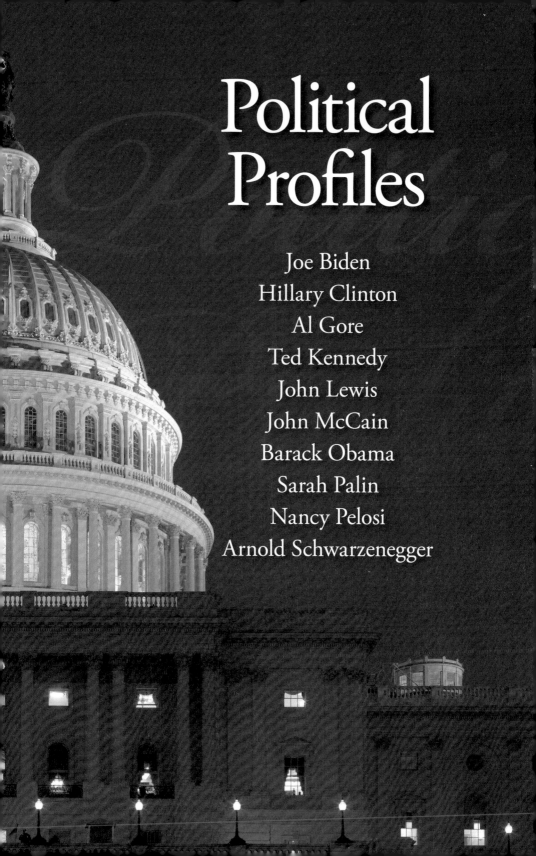

Political Profiles

Joe Biden

Hillary Clinton

Al Gore

Ted Kennedy

John Lewis

John McCain

Barack Obama

Sarah Palin

Nancy Pelosi

Arnold Schwarzenegger

Political Profiles: Sarah Palin

Library of Congress Cataloging-in-Publication Data

Petrillo, Lisa.
Political profiles : Sarah Palin / by Lisa Petrillo. -- 1st ed.
p. cm.
ISBN 978-1-59935-133-9 (alk. paper)
1. Palin, Sarah, 1964---Juvenile literature. 2. Women
governors--Alaska--Biography--Juvenile literature. 3.
Governors--Alaska--Biography--Juvenile literature. I. Title.
F910.7.P35P48 2009
973.931092--dc22
[B]

2009040834

Printed in the United States of America
First Edition

To Bob, Clark, and Ava, who bring sweetness to life

Sunset at Juneau harbor, Alaska

Contents

Sarah Palin with Republican presidential candidate
John McCain at the Republican National Convention in
Minneapolis-St. Paul, Minnesota, on September 3, 2008.

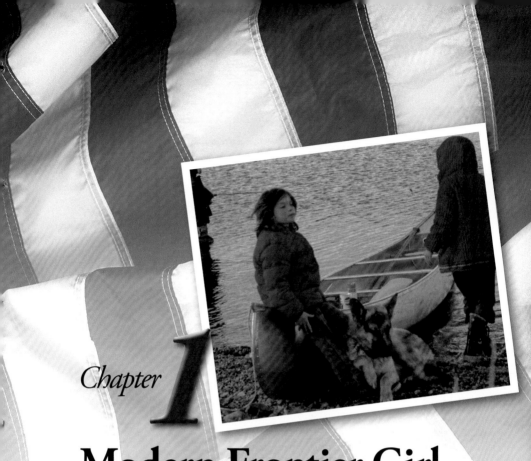

Chapter

1

Modern Frontier Girl

S arah Palin learned to shoot when she was eight years old. By age ten she had bagged her first kill, a rabbit. This meant she beat out folk hero Daniel Boone, the American pioneer, who according to legend didn't start hunting until he was twelve. In Sarah Palin's Alaskan childhood, growing up hunting was normal, and in the Palin family it was expected. The daughter of a hard-driving father, Palin was pushed to work hard and to be fearless when pursuing a goal, two traits that have helped her meteoric political career.

Sarah Louise Heath was born February 11, 1964, in Sandpoint, Idaho. She was the third of four children of Sally and Charles

(Chuck) Heath, a popular schoolteacher and coach. Sandpoint sat near the U.S.-Canadian border in an area renowned for its pristine lakes and stunning mountains. But Chuck Heath wanted bigger frontiers—and a bigger paycheck. A few hundred miles northwest of his hometown sat the vast and mostly unsettled Alaska, which had officially become a U.S. state five years before. Statehood was attracting lots of new residents, and the new state needed more teachers to handle its growing schools and offered experienced teachers bigger salaries to move there.

Alaska is so vast it can swallow California and Texas and have room left over for Montana. Sarah's father was so determined to live in America's last frontier, even an earthquake couldn't shake his resolve. In March 1964, an 8.4 magnitude quake struck Alaska, killing more than 110 people. Yet soon after, Chuck moved the Heath family to Skagway, a remote old gold-rush town.

After gold had been discovered in the Yukon Territory at the turn of the twentieth century, Skagway became a rowdy lawless boomtown. But soon the gold and the boom ended. When the Heath family arrived a few decades later, less than seven hundred people lived there.

Sarah's family spent five years in Skagway. She arrived as an infant along with her brother Chuck Jr., age two, and sister Heather, who was one. Another sibling, Molly, was born in Skagway.

Sarah's father taught school and took odd jobs, including driving taxicabs for the summer tourists. Sarah's mother also worked several jobs.

Chuck Heath took his kids fishing, hunting for goats and seals, and prospecting for old gold-mining relics. The family's hunting and fishing excursions were not just great adventure;

they provided meat for the dinner table along with the giant garden that the kids helped farm.

Chuck mounted his game trophies all over the house and yard: caribou, moose, bear, sheep, and mountain goats. Pelts were proudly laid over chairs and couches. On their frequent family hikes, he would point out geological formations and vegetation of interest, and quiz the children later on what they had seen. "Dad never stopped lining up new adventures for us," said Sarah's big brother, Chuck Jr.

Sarah was an adventurous tomboy, never afraid to get dirty or play cowboys and Indians. One of her most remarkable characteristics was her stubbornness. When her mind was made up, even her strong-minded father couldn't shake her. "The rest of the kids, I could force them to do something," Chuck Heath recalled. "But with Sarah, there was no way. From a young age

Sarah, center, with her brother
Chuck and sister Heather

she had a mind of her own. Once she made up her mind, she didn't change it."

With little access to TV because of the remote location, the children made their own entertainment. Sometimes they would gather around the Heath's wood-burning stove that heated the house, and Sarah's father would break out the boxing gloves. He would referee boxing matches between his kids and neighbor children. Sarah boxed both girls and boys. "She was a tough little girl," recalled family friend Paul Moore.

Anchorage on an April evening

In 1969, the Heath family left remote Skagway and moved to the city of Anchorage, where they at first stayed with relatives of one of Chuck Heath's old high school football buddies. When Sarah's father landed a job in nearby Eagle River they got their own place.

Two years later the Heath family moved again, this time for good. They settled in Wasilla, a small town of about four hundred people located about forty miles from Anchorage. Wasilla had started out as a railroad outpost for miners and fur-trap-

pers, and became a farming settlement during the Great Depression. One of the many solutions that then-President Franklin Roosevelt came up with to solve the terrible poverty facing America was to send starving farmers from the scorched Southwest to settle in areas such as Wasilla.

The town was located in a valley surrounded by two mountain ranges, with deep forests of birch and spruce trees. There were also lakes where Sarah would swim, despite water so frigid it turned her skin blue.

Wasilla was the population center for the Matanuska-Susitna Borough (a borough is similar to a county) in a valley the size of the state of West Virginia. Its mountains stand as the gateway to the spectacular Denali National Park, where Chuck loved to take the family camping—and where once they had a potentially fatal encounter with a bear.

When Sarah was nine, her hometown became the starting point for the Iditarod, a famous and challenging sled dog race that lasted seventeen days across the frozen tundra. Her school was even named for the big festival-filled event: Iditarod Elementary.

The next year, 1974, Wasilla formed itself into a full-fledged city and the population started increasing from the few hundred into the thousands. The Heaths lived close to the center of town. The family had a white cat named Fifi and a German shepherd named Rufus for pets. Sarah and her two sisters shared an attic bedroom heated only by a wood stove downstairs. When it got really cold, one of the girls would call out the code word, Sleeping Beauty, and they'd all pile into one bed for warmth.

The four Heath children were expected to do chores, such as stacking firewood, gutting and cleaning fish, and dressing wild game to ready it for the family dinner table. Then they cleaned the supper dishes afterward. The children also helped to tend the garden that helped to sustain them when the gro-

The house Sarah lived in with her family in Wasilla

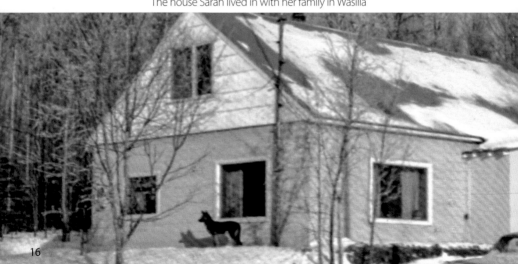

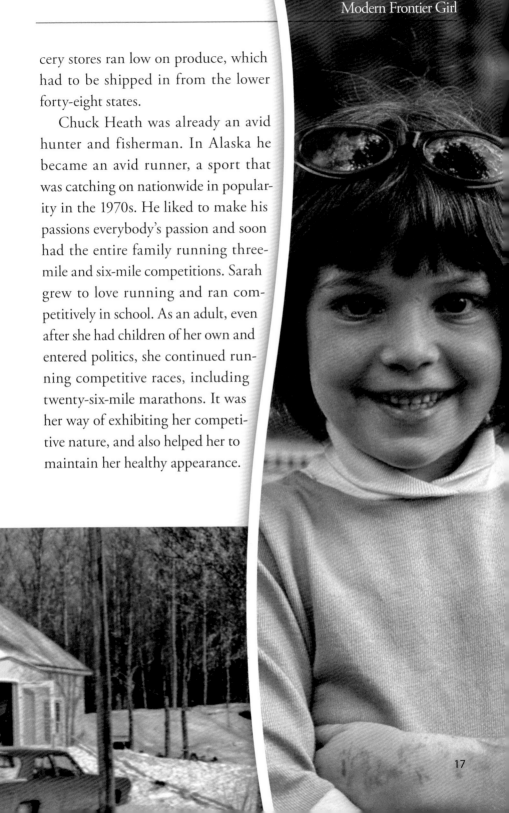

cery stores ran low on produce, which had to be shipped in from the lower forty-eight states.

Chuck Heath was already an avid hunter and fisherman. In Alaska he became an avid runner, a sport that was catching on nationwide in popularity in the 1970s. He liked to make his passions everybody's passion and soon had the entire family running three-mile and six-mile competitions. Sarah grew to love running and ran competitively in school. As an adult, even after she had children of her own and entered politics, she continued running competitive races, including twenty-six-mile marathons. It was her way of exhibiting her competitive nature, and also helped her to maintain her healthy appearance.

Sarah, left, with a table of
ptarmigan her family shot in Alaska

Chapter **2**

Miss Congeniality

W hile Sarah's father was the master outdoorsman, her mother Sally was the master of the home arts. She ran the household with a gentle hand and was skillful at keeping the peace among sometimes squabbling siblings. She was a working mother, serving as the Wasilla school secretary. She was known widely for her kindness and her talent for putting people at ease.

Sarah absorbed her father's competitive nature, and learned much from her mother's charm. Both would serve her well in her climb to the top in the rough game of politics.

Sarah's mother was deeply religious. Sally believed in a more structured path to spiritual enlightenment. She had her children baptized as Roman Catholics and they attended mass faithfully. After settling in Wasilla, she started attending with her children the Wasilla Assembly of God, a Pentecostal church. Pentecostals believe the Bible is the actual word of God; they follow the word

Sarah, right, with her sisters, Heather, center, and Molly on the left

literally in order to make it into heaven when the end time, the apocalypse, arrives.

Worshippers sometimes would get so worked up they would burst into strange languages, a practice called speaking in tongues. Their belief is that the spirit of God had entered them and caused them to shout out. The Pentecostal church became a major part of their life, with Sunday services as well as Wednesday night devotions, potluck suppers, socializing, card games, and lots of youth activities, including summer Bible camp. The Assembly of God's pastors became a big part of Sarah's spiritual development.

When Sarah was twelve, her pastor dunked her completely into the frigid Little Beaver Lake along with her mother and siblings. They experienced the traditional full-immersion baptism, a ceremony that in their religion means they were "born again" as Christians. Religious zeal filled Sarah so strongly that she felt compelled to openly share her beliefs publicly throughout her life. She signed her friends' yearbooks with Bible verses.

Her religious belief led Sarah to her first political win. She was voted president of Wasilla High's Fellowship of Christian Athletes. Sarah would later say that she entered politics because she felt it was God's plan for her to govern.

Her faith helped her through her sometimes painful adolescence. In junior high, she was still an awkward tomboy stuck with thick glasses and an unflattering haircut. She developed a crush on the most popular boy in school and became upset that he chose for his girlfriend someone more talented and prettier. It was painful to witness her jealousy, recalled the girl much later, "I could tell it was eating her up. I couldn't relate to wanting anything that badly—to be first, to get the guy, to get the highest score, that you could be sick with it."

The success of Sarah's older siblings overshadowed her during her junior high years. Chuck Jr. was so talented athletically he went on to play football for University of Idaho. Big sister Heather was captain of the varsity basketball team; she became a local hero when her team qualified for the state championships two years running.

Determined Sarah kept plugging, and her hard work helped her come out of the shadows and blossom by the middle of high school. She joined lots of clubs and competed in three sports: track, cross-country running, and basketball. On the basketball court, she played so aggressively she earned the nickname "Barracuda."

When Sarah was in eleventh grade, she expected to be promoted to the prestigious varsity basketball squad. However, her coaches told her she wasn't good enough yet. She was bitterly disappointed to be held back in junior varsity.

In her senior year in Wasilla High, a new boy named Todd Palin arrived. Todd was a talented athlete who had grown up in a remote fishing village some two hundred miles outside Anchorage.

His Eskimo ancestors had passed on their hard-to-get commercial fishing license to him, which meant he was a go-getter who already had a livelihood. He was tall and handsome and had his own car, plus a truck and a boat. Girls swooned over him, but it was Sarah who beat out all the other competition to capture his heart.

"He was the best basketball player I had ever seen," Sarah said later. Todd for his part would say she caught his eye as the best-looking girl on her team.

Because Alaska is so big and its weather so severe, being a high school athlete meant students rode buses for hours to play a rival high school. Then after the game, the teams would camp out in an empty school classroom before playing another game the next day and then taking the long bus ride home. Girls and boys teams rode together on these weekend-long road trips. In such a close atmosphere, friendships and romances often flourish, as with Sarah and Todd.

By her senior year of high school, Sarah rose to become varsity basketball co-captain. The Wasilla Warriors continued on their winning streak. "Barracuda" was determined to be part of the team's success, but near the end of the regular season she hurt her ankle. A doctor warned her that if she didn't sit out the upcoming state championship tournament, she risked damaging her ankle permanently. But Sarah refused to be benched. She played on through the pain.

The final championship game pitted her three hundred-student Warriors against a big-city Anchorage school with 2,000 students. The event drew thousands of fans, including Sarah's family plus Todd, now officially her boyfriend. He starred on the boy's basketball team that also reached the state tournament, but they had finished in fourth place.

In the second half of Sarah's big game, the coach benched her because her bad ankle was hurting her game. In the last quarter when the Warriors had a comfortable nine-point lead, their opponents started catching up. An already exciting and close game reached fever pitch.

Soon Sarah's team was winning by only four points. This worried the coaches and crowd because basketball is such a fast and intense game that in less than a minute, a team that is a four-point leader can become a two-point loser. The coach put Sarah back in the game, with the strategy to get the other team to foul Sarah. Then she could go to the free-throw line and score. With only thirty seconds left in the championship game, Sarah successfully drew a foul, and her big chance. Sarah remained cool despite the pressure and scored the important extra point. She had also sustained a stress fracture in her ankle. Wasilla won, 58-53.

It was the Warriors' first championship. The play and the game were so important to Sarah she would talk about it publicly for years to come. In speeches she would often say that on the basketball court she had learned about how to succeed in life—the game taught her humility, how to triumph over adversity, and the importance of having talented people at your side.

"I know this sounds hokey, but basketball was a life-changing experience for me. It's all about setting a goal, about discipline, teamwork, and then success."

Also life changing was her romance with high school sweetheart Todd. He took her on dates snowmobiling. They went to the senior prom together. The summer after graduation, Sarah joined Todd on Bristol Bay to help him during the short and grueling commercial fishing season. It was hard and

Sarah, number twenty-two, was a point guard for her high school during the 1982 state basketball championship sometimes dangerous work under harsh Alaskan weather conditions. Sarah proved to Todd that she could be a true partner, not just the prettiest girl on the team bus.

Todd had grown up in a small village of 2,400 so remote it could be reached only by boat or sky. He is part Eskimo, and was close to his grandmother who was a respected elder among the Yu'pik native people. His parents divorced when he was young, and he remained in his hometown with her, his two siblings, and his stepfather, who ran the town hardware store. When Todd was a teenager, he and a sibling moved to the Alaska interior to live with their father, Jim Palin, who had remarried. His father was also athletic, and was a well-known basketball referee.

In 1981, Todd's last year in high school, his father took a job with a regional electric company. His new job took him to Wasilla, where he joined local organizations to get to know the townspeople.

In school Sarah always knew she needed a college degree to fulfill her ambition to have a career. She dreamed of being a sports news announcer for ESPN, a national cable sports channel. She earned good grades but not outstanding ones. College would prove to be challenging for her.

She and three close high school friends applied to college together. Instead of choosing a university based on its academics, Sarah and her friends chose on the basis of geography: they wanted someplace warm that was easy enough that they could all get accepted despite their scholastic records. They chose the University of Hawaii at Hilo.

But they forgot to do their homework about their choice. Sarah had visited her aunt on Oahu once, so she thought she knew Hawaii. Hilo is exotic and beautiful but it is not the picture-postcard Hawaii. It sits on the rainy and rugged side of the

Big Island where it rained and rained on them. The four Alaskan teenagers became so discouraged, so quickly, that they withdrew from college.

Sarah refused to admit defeat so easily. Two of the friends moved back to Alaska, while she and another friend transferred to the private Hawaii Pacific University on Oahu. There, they were finally living in the warm tropical magnificence of postcard-perfect island life. They lived on their own off campus near the beach, but they missed the camaraderie of school life. They went home for winter break, and in the spring enrolled in North Idaho College, a junior college that offered job training and two-year degrees only. From there, Sarah decided she was ready for more challenging academics and a traditional college scene, so she transferred to the University of Idaho, a comprehensive four-year university with advanced degree programs. Her brother played on the university football team. First, however, Sarah took a break from college to work and earn money for school. She moved back home and found a job as an office receptionist.

Back in Wasilla she ran into one of the politically connected Republicans in the area. The woman was also the mother of the boy she had had such a crush on in junior high. The woman and her husband ran the local beauty pageant, and she became an important mentor for Sarah by grooming her for the Miss America contest. Sarah learned poise and presentation; she got a complete beauty makeover and glamorous clothes. For her talent demonstration in the pageant, Sarah played the flute as she had in school.

The now transformed Sarah won the Miss Wasilla crown and qualified for the next step, the Miss Alaska contest. If she won that beauty pageant, she could move up to compete in the national pageant whose winners often went on to become famous.

Her brother teased his tomboy sister about being a beauty queen, but she responded that she was going to win scholarship money for college. Sarah came in second in the Miss Alaska contest, but scored her scholarship and the prize of Miss Congeniality.

In addition, she discovered that she loved being on stage. The pageant rekindled that feeling of admiration from the crowd that she had experienced in those champion-ship Wasilla High basketball games.

What would prove even more important to Sarah's future was that she had forged her first political connections in the Republican Party. It was a pattern she would repeat successfully all the way to the top.

A 1984 studio portrait of Sarah

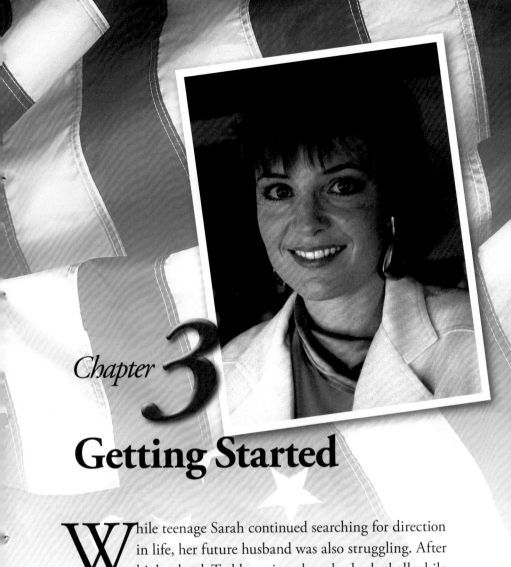

Chapter 3

Getting Started

While teenage Sarah continued searching for direction in life, her future husband was also struggling. After high school, Todd continued to play basketball while taking classes at a nearby community college and then the state university. His former high school coach recruited him to play in a small college in Missouri. But despite Todd's strong work ethic, he proved no match for college players who were bigger, faster, and more worldly. And he was finding it unbearably hot outside his beloved Alaska. Todd left school and never earned a college degree.

That same year, Sarah was flush from the pageant and from earning her own paycheck. At the academically challenging University of Idaho, she studied communications, specializing in broadcast journalism. On her dorm wall she hung a poster of Libby Riddles, the first woman to win the Iditarod, the famous sled-dog race across Alaska.

In fall 1985, she returned home and took a few lower-cost courses at Matanuski-Susitna Community College. She then returned to the University of Idaho. After spending five years at five colleges, she earned a bachelor's degree in journalism in 1987.

Her first job was as an intern with the local newspaper, the *Mat-Su Valley Frontiersman*, which published three times a week. Then she landed a job as a sports reporter for an NBC affiliate station in Anchorage. She finally had a job that put her where she wanted to be, on television and in the public eye. Sarah felt proud that she finally was on her way. She moved in with older sister Heather in an apartment in Alaska's biggest city.

Todd was still struggling. He still had his commercial fishing work every June and July during the season. And, during Alaska's long winters he worked driving snowplows. He had run into trouble a few months earlier while hanging out with his buddies; he was charged with breaking drunk driving laws at age twenty-two.

For Alaskan kids, one of the biggest events of the year was the state fair with all its bright lights, fun food, and diversions. On August 29, 1988, Sarah and Todd went to the Alaska State Fair with Heather. The group split up, arranging to meet later for the ride home together.

When the appointed meeting time came, Heather couldn't find them so she left without them. To everyone's surprise, what Sarah and Todd did instead was take the ultimate wild ride—

they got married. They had secretly slipped away to a nearby courthouse and roused the justice of the peace. The young couple was so unprepared they didn't have the necessary witnesses. So they ran to a nearby nursing home and brought back two elderly people, one in a wheelchair and another with a walker, to make the marriage legal. Sarah Palin was twenty-four.

Todd moved in with the sisters in their apartment while he waited to hear about his application for one of the prized Alaska blue-collar jobs, working for the giant oil companies. The oil industry was Alaska's biggest, with many profitable international corporations drilling and extracting the state's sizable oil and natural gas resources. Working conditions were hard, but the pay was excellent.

In April 1989, eight months after their elopement, their first child was born. They named their son Track because he was born during track season.

Just before their son was born, Palin and Todd bought their first home, a condominium. Todd had gotten hired by British Petroleum, and became one of the thousands of oil workers who work twelve-hour shifts in seven or fourteen day rotations. His schedule was either seven days at work with seven days off back home, or two weeks away from home and then two weeks off. His job was protected by a labor union, which provided a contract guaranteeing health insurance benefits, paid vacation days, and strong job security. Oil workers have to leave their hometowns and families and perform hard and sometimes dangerous work. Crews fly out of local airports on charter planes to Prudhoe Bay, a ninety-minute flight from Anchorage. They live in barracks run by the oil companies, which resemble upscale military bases complete with swimming pools, gyms, basketball and volleyball courts, movie theaters, TVs, and cafeterias.

After having their first baby, Palin returned to work at another Anchorage TV station, covering high school sports. It was a small station where she got experience performing many aspects of news production, both in front of and behind the camera. These would prove important skills for someone like Palin, who was determined to live in the public eye. Soon she became pregnant with their second child, a daughter, born in February 1990. They named her Bristol, after the salmon-filled Alaskan bay off of the Bering Sea where Todd ran his fishing business.

Palin's hands were full caring for two babies both still in diapers. She had the option now to quit work and stay home with the kids, since the couple was financially stable thanks to Todd's steady paycheck, supplemented with his annual fishing money. He typically hauls in some 60,000 pounds of salmon per season, in some years earning around $45,000.

Now she was a stay-at-home mom with more time on her hands. Palin turned her energy toward serious training as a runner. Her father had run in the famed twenty-six-mile-long Boston Marathon. Not to be outdone, she began training and running so many miles she sometimes ran to the next town and back. She joined a local gym and became a regular at aerobics dance exercise classes. Her gym experience connected her with other fitness-oriented women she bonded with. She formed a group with other young mothers who got so expert at aerobics dancing they performed publicly. They called themselves the Elite Six. The women all came from different backgrounds, religions, and political beliefs. They provided an important social outlet for Palin and also helped broaden her circle.

Aerobics exercise classes revolve around dance-like movements set to high-energy music; it's a full-body workout that leaves participants feeling energized. One of her exercise classmates was John Stein, Wasilla's longtime mayor. He noticed Palin in the class and was impressed by her energy and charm. He mentioned her to his friend Nick Carney.

Carney already knew Palin's family. He had an extensive background in state and local government. He had served as a high-placed state official and then moved back to his hometown of Wasilla to run his own garbage-collection business.

Stein and Carney decided Palin would be an ideal recruit to help them with their campaign to move the city of Wasilla to the next level. They became her political godfathers, the important first step to propel her into professional-level politics.

The Parks Highway, which connects Anchorage to Fairbanks, runs through downtown Wasilla.

Wasilla had a problem. The small city sat in the midst of a sprawling rural borough where the center of political power was—similar to a county with a county seat. Most major government services like schools, law enforcement, and environmental protections were outside the city of Wasilla's control, because they were run by the borough or state. Law enforcement in the mostly rural Alaska is generally run by the state troopers. Troopers are typically spread thin over such a large area.

Wasilla's mayor and his friend Carney wanted the city to create its own police force. With a local police force, residents would get more protection and it would attract more businesses that

preferred having an available police force to keep theft down and handle other emergencies more quickly.

They needed money to start a force from scratch, to buy squad cars, headquarters, guns, uniforms, and a police radio system. Mayor Stein and Carney wanted to impose a 2 percent sales tax on the town to provide the funding for the police force. The way it would work was to charge people two cents per dollar they spent buying things. The tax, like all taxes, would go to the needs that all citizens share, such as roads and water systems. Palin liked the idea of seeing her hometown grow and gain big-city advantages.

They agreed to help each other. She would join their cause and campaign to get support from fellow fundamentalist Christians and fellow parents she knew from her kids' sports leagues. In exchange, they would become her political mentors and back her candidacy for the Wasilla City Council.

And so at age twenty-eight, Sarah Palin entered politics.

Chapter 4

Learning the Political Game

As a politician, Palin had to start from scratch. She had no money to campaign, so she used her best assets: her beauty, her charm, and her family connections. Everyone in the valley seemed to know her dad Chuck, the hunter and fisherman who had taught science to and coached generations of kids at Wasilla High. Likewise, Sally Heath was well known for her kindness both at school and at church.

Still, Wasilla was a far different place than when Palin's family arrived more than twenty years before. Then there were four hundred people, now there were more than 4,000. It helped her campaign to have the popular and well-known Carney at her side, as Palin started walking door-to-door to introduce herself as a candidate. She would pull her children Track and Bristol along in a wagon as she campaigned.

In the fall 1992 election both Carney and Palin won seats on the City Council. Now the tax-for-cops group had a solid majority to push through its ambitious plans.

Palin's political godfather, Carney possessed an impressive background. He had grown up in Wasilla when Alaska was still a U.S. territory. He left for the East Coast to earn his college degree from the prestigious Dartmouth College in New Hampshire. He then returned to work in Juneau, Alaska's capital.

His career included working for the state to develop economic opportunities, and serving as Alaska's agriculture director, so he had experience at high levels in government and business. On a personal level Carney was close to Palin's in-laws. He was such a sports fan, he served as a basketball referee like Todd's father, Jim.

With Palin immersed in her newfound passion, politics, Todd launched a new passion of his own: becoming a professional snowmobile racer. Snowmobiles, which Alaskans refer to as snow machines, are small, motorized boatlike vessels that roar across snow atop skis and treads. In February 1993, Todd entered his first Iron Dog, a nearly 2,000-mile multiday snowmobile race across the windy arctic tundra. Racers competed for prize purses that topped $25,000. It became an expensive and time-consuming pastime. The training and the race itself took Todd

Vehicles on the Parks Highway in downtown Wasilla, Alaska

away from the family. So did his oil-field job, and his summer commercial fishing work. The couple was lucky to have a strong network of family and friends to help care for their small children while they focused on their separate personal challenges.

The Palin family stayed very busy, especially with Todd now working three jobs. To support his racing, Todd launched another side business, opening a shop that sold and repaired snowmobiles. Palin also took on many duties by joining the school Parent Teacher Association, and she ferried Track to ice hockey and Bristol to soccer and basketball. Plus, Palin continued to help Todd with his commercial fishing in June and July. One fishing season, when she was twenty-nine, her fingers got crushed out on the boat. After getting treatment at the local hospital, she was back out on the boat helping the next day, saying she didn't want to disappoint Todd.

Fishing is serious business in Alaska. Commercial fishing permits are limited in Todd's hometown of Dillingham, to protect such vital natural resources as Bristol Bay from being ruined by overfishing. During the 1993 fishing season, Palin got caught running afoul of the fishing laws. She fished without having the proper fishing license, and pleaded no contest in local court, agreeing to take punishment without argument. The crime was a minor one, a misdemeanor, but the violation was mistakenly recorded as a felony. This mistake would later cost her dearly.

Just after Independence Day 1994 Palin gave birth to the couple's third child, Willow. Palin seemed to be living a charmed life. She had found her life's calling in politics, a business she had gotten into easily. She had freely found mentors to teach her the ropes. She shined in the public eye, and people knew her everywhere. Her work gave her a flexible schedule, and her family network provided plenty of help with free childcare. Now she'd had another easy childbirth. As always, Palin returned to her work quickly and then easily won reelection to a second City Council term.

What was not easy was Palin's relationship with the majority on the City Council. After absorbing the guidance of her two political godfathers for the first eighteen months, Palin began to break away. She became outspokenly critical of the way they ran the city. She reacted against them like they were holding her back on the political junior varsity. She wanted to not only move up to varsity, she wanted to be captain of the team—Wasilla's mayor.

"Mayor Stein and Nick Carney told me, 'You'll learn quick, just listen to us.' Well, they didn't know how I was wired."

Only the toughest politicians can stomach the idea of knocking down friends and climbing over them to get to the top politically. Palin had already proven tough in a physical game like basketball. This election would prove her genius in the political game as well.

Her problem was this: how could a novice like her beat a popular and experienced three-term mayor whose progressive ideas literally transformed the city? Mayor Stein's sales tax gamble brought a new police force that was reducing crime and attracting more businesses, including a Walmart. The city treasury was overflowing, and Wasilla continued to grow with more residents and businesses to keep the coffers full. Soon it would become Alaska's fourth-largest city.

Because of Stein, Wasilla's civic success was bucking the national trend. In the early 1990s, an economic recession was crippling business and government alike. The recession followed years of government overspending and debt expansion. In 1993 populist Democrat Bill Clinton was elected president, and he blamed the 1990-91 recession on twelve years of "trickle down economics" started under the administration of Ronald Reagan.

While Palin was learning the ropes in grassroots politics in the farthest corner of America, President Clinton was successfully reversing the national economic decline. He would soon balance the federal budget for the first time in three decades.

In nonpartisan elections like the Wasilla City Council, what matters to local voters generally is not political ideology but day-to-day practicality: who is going to fix the roads and do something about their neighbor's barking dog?

Palin turned that standard wisdom on its head. For the 1996 mayor's race she courted the state Republican Party, finding powerful mentors to help her win the mayor's race. She had been making a name for herself as a politician unafraid to confront the powerful, and one proud to flaunt her conservative beliefs despite what mainstream voters might think. Republican Party leaders saw in her someone they could work with to increase their power base.

Palin was learning that in the art of politics, perception can become reality. She took her cues from the national Republican Party leaders who had gained a huge following and a majority in the U.S. Congress by demonizing Democrats with slogans and nicknames like "tax and spend liberals"—even if it wasn't true.

Palin painted herself as a conservative and her opponent as a liberal money-waster. She argued with Stein on how to spend the city's $4 million budget surplus. His projects and proposals she labeled wasteful, and she maintained that the city needed to cut spending drastically despite its rapid growth and its overflowing treasury.

"John would have all of us believe that every one of us is eager for Wasilla to become a 'mini-Anchorage,' building new facilities, increasing taxes, and restricting our uniquely Alaskan way of life," she told a group of Wasilla business people. "There is a colossal difference between John Stein and me. I'm a conservative and he's a liberal. A good-old-boy politician."

Religion also figured into the race. Palin was billed as "Wasilla's first Christian mayor." It was a good slogan to motivate voters among the large local population of evangelicals. But it wasn't true that Stein was a liberal or a non-Christian. Like Palin, he was a registered Republican and had been raised as a Lutheran, which is a mainstream Christian religion. She astutely appealed to the rise of a different brand of Christians, the conservative evangelicals and fundamentalists whose movement into politics had grown so powerful since the 1980s that one of its leaders, Pat Robertson, ran for U.S. president under the Republican Party banner.

The national GOP succeeded in blocking President Clinton's ambitious agenda of health-care expansion and educational programs aimed at improving the economy and lifting millions out of poverty. The potent Republican backlash to President Clinton was mostly powered by the GOP tapping the anger and frustration of the working class and religious community.

In the 1990s, millions of American workers were losing their jobs as big multinational companies shipped work overseas to low-wage workers in Third World countries. Many in the religious community had shunned politics until their leaders convinced them that America was in a culture war, and that the values they held dear were being pushed to the very edge of a cliff and would disappear unless they acted. In both cases of the culture wars and the economic decline, many Republican and

religious leaders were blaming liberal Democrats as the enemy, the ones pushing those values off the cliff. By 1994 politics and religion were mixing so openly that voting guides were often distributed in churches.

Palin didn't have to fake her evangelical credentials. She had remained deeply part of the fundamentalist Christian com-

munity. She was encouraged by the success of mixing partisan politics with biblical beliefs, and she started talking about the bigger hot-button national issues in her campaign, even though they had little to do with the mayor's office. Bigger issues like less restrictive gun laws meant more attention and bigger endorsements—her campaign bore the names of well-known national and statewide groups and politicians.

"She ran on issues that had nothing to do with the city," Carney said. "We were all about preserving the lakes and improving highways and maybe joining Palmer (a nearby city) to share services—the library was overloaded and inadequate—and those issues should have captured the campaign."

'ASILLA CITY HALL

EXIT ONLY

One national issue that influenced the race was abortion. The medical procedure has been legal in the United States since 1973, but it was also one of the most hotly debated issues in the nation. Palin opposed abortion even if the girl or woman was a crime victim and had become pregnant through rape by a stranger or by a family member. Palin won endorsements based on her stance. But once she entered the national political scene her abortion views were considered controversial, as more extreme than those of the majority of Americans.

Censorship was another controversial issue in Palin's career that reflected her newfound evangelical brand of political activism. In her run-up to the mayor's race, Palin had publicly taken a stand in the City Council about possibly banning a library book called *Daddy's Roommate*. The 1991 children's book featured a boy's positive experience with his divorced father and the dad's gay partner. The evangelical community in many pockets of the nation held this book up as an example of their moral values coming under attack, for they believed homosexuality to be sinful and not to be encouraged in library books. From 1990 to 2000 and beyond, *Daddy's Roommate* has been one of the most censorship-challenged books in the nation, according to the American Library Association.

Palin tangled with the city's quiet and respected librarian who publicly refused to censor it or any book. Palin's closest ally on the Wasilla Council didn't back up her challenge. Instead, Councilwoman Laura Chase read the book and praised it as sensitive and appropriate. Chase suggested every councilmember read it, especially Palin, and was shocked when her friend seemed horrified at the idea. Censorship would be revisited again in Palin's career.

The mayoral race excited Wasilla's populace and divided it as well. Palin's first race for City Council in 1992 drew 840 total voters. In her reelection less than six hundred people voted. The 1996 mayoral race drew 1,091 voters total, with Palin winning with 651 votes.

One night before that fateful election Palin stayed up late talking intimately with her friend and campaign manager, her fellow councilwoman Chase. Chase thought she was being daring by suggesting that things were going so well for Palin that at this rate she might be able to run for governor in another ten years.

Thirty-two-year-old Palin responded, "I want to be president."

Chapter **5**

Hardball

Winning was everything. Palin had grown up in a house with a father who pushed his kids to excel. And Palin did win: the state basketball championship, the high school hero, the beauty pageant, and every political race she had entered.

Ironically, Palin had won office by pledging to cut government spending. Yet the man she defeated, Mayor Stein, had saved the city money because he was capable of doing two jobs for the price of one. For twelve years Stein served as both mayor and city manager of Wasilla, since he had the business and managerial experience and a university degree in public administration to guide him.

After Palin took over the mayor's office, she hired a full-time city manager at $50,000 a year, to take care of the thousands of details about roads and sewers and contracts needed to run a city. Her critics howled this was proof that Palin was not ready for the job. Her choice for the job was not her friend and campaign manager Chase, who claimed Palin had promised her the job. Instead, Palin gave the job to an aide of a powerful Republican legislator, someone with political connections.

In Wasilla, business continued to flourish and fill the city treasury, allowing Palin to fulfill her campaign promise to cut taxes. She started by cutting her own salary from $68,000 to $64,200 per year, although technically her self-imposed pay cut couldn't take effect for quite some time.

Her first move was to shake up city hall. She told city executives she expected utmost loyalty—essentially, they were either with her or they were against her. "Wasilla is moving forward in a positive direction. This is the time for the department heads to let me know if they plan to move forward or if it's time for a change," she said.

So startled were the townspeople by her governing style that the local newspaper, the *Frontiersman*, criticized her for confusing her election with a "coronation."

The library director fired back. Right before the December holidays, the *Frontiersman* featured a story that the new mayor was advocating banning books that offended her religious beliefs. Librarian Mary Ellen Emmons said that "the free exchange of information is my job, and I will fight anyone who tries to interfere with that."

Palin disputed the censorship claim in the newspaper. She admitted she had held multiple discussions with the librarian but she considered them general or "rhetorical."

Emmons was a respected professional who served as the head of the Alaska Library Association. She disagreed with Palin's view that their discussions were merely rhetorical, saying in the town newspaper, "This is different than a normal book selection procedure or a book challenge policy. She asked me if I would object to censorship and I replied, 'Yup.' And I told her it would not be just me. This was a constitutional question.'"

This scuffle over censorship would grow in importance as Palin sought higher office. Many questioned whether she would uphold democracy of all the people, when she had apparently made attempts to suppress it. Palin soon fired the librarian who had publicly declared she would fight censorship.

The librarian's firing created widespread community uproar. Within a day, Palin was forced to retreat and rehire her. None of the other department heads were as lucky.

Palin fired the police chief, who had been her friend and who had created the department. He sued, eventually losing his court case against the city. Palin asked for the resignation of the director of the city's pioneer museum as well. The director had ambitious plans to expand the museum and its role as a regional cultural center. Palin suffered some controversy when her museum budget-cutting resulted in three beloved museum staff members quitting in protest. One of those who quit was an elderly woman who had been an early pioneer to the town herself.

Palin fired the city's attorney, and replaced him with a lawyer who had served as attorney for the Alaska Republican Party.

The local newspapers reported heavily on the controversy and turmoil from her major changes. So she banned city employees from talking to the press without permission. Reporters were furious that she was limiting constitutional rights to free speech. A group of townspeople were so alarmed at Palin's actions they

A view of homes and a birch forest near Wasilla

announced they were going to fire the mayor, and they started organizing for a recall election to unseat her.

Palin realized she needed to make peace with the media, so she charmed them back into her corner with bouquets of flowers as apologies, and inviting them to lunch where she explained her point of view. It worked. Palin's governing style was bold and her moves often controversial, so the media would continue to occasionally criticize. But the papers backed off from the constant negative coverage. And the townspeople who proposed firing her through an election recall decided they didn't want a fight with someone nicknamed the Barracuda. They decided it was wiser to give her a chance.

Palin succeeded in forcefully showing the town she would not accept business as usual. She would sum up her philosophy of governing: "I didn't get into government to do the safe and easy things. A ship in harbor is safe, but that's not why the ship is built."

Most of her changes stuck. One of the few plans that failed was when she tried installing her hand-selected backers on the city council, so she would have enjoyed a clear majority to endorse her new policies. Fellow council members however pushed back, declaring her move a violation of city law. One of Palin's proposed appointees was an activist with the Alaska Independence Party. The Independence Party was a controversial political party that advocated taking Alaska out of the United States. The activist had donated heavily to her campaign and worked hard to get her elected, helping deliver a lot of conservative votes her way.

Since Palin had dismissed most of the heads of departments without lining up replacements, the city had no police chief for months. Her choice was a man without the experience of Wasilla's first police chief, who had worked twenty-two years on the Anchorage force. The new chief Duwayne "Charlie" Fannon had only run a rural force half the size of Wasilla. Philosophically, he was more in tune with Palin's conservative viewpoints. As he told the city council, he was a law enforcement officer who believed having too many laws restricted people's freedom.

To make peace with the community, Palin started a new tradition in town of throwing a civic Christmas party, complete with a Christmas-tree lighting ceremony. Despite the rough start, Palin learned the ropes quickly. In her first term she made major moves to keep pace with growth. With her push, voters approved a $5.5 million bond to pave roads. Municipal bonds are loans that public agencies take out to pay for big building projects, and like most loans require payback with extra fees and interest paid off. All this public spending loaded public debt into the city budget, Palin's persistent critics pointed out. But what voters and businesses saw, they liked—especially when Mayor Palin lowered taxes on personal property, business inventory, and aircraft taxes.

One small disaster confronted her when the winter of 1998 was snowless again. This meant a big loss to Wasilla, which had

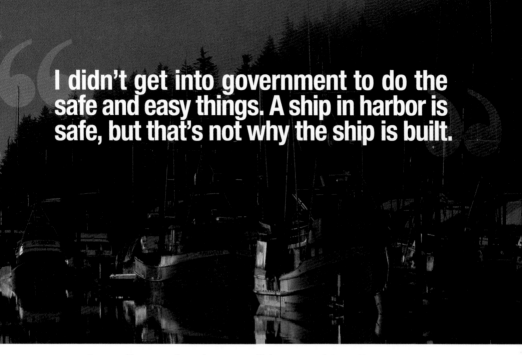

> I didn't get into government to do the safe and easy things. A ship in harbor is safe, but that's not why the ship is built.

traditionally served as the start of the annual Iron Dog snowmobile race as well as the Iditarod sled-dog race. There seemed to be a trend of regionwide warming. It was the third time in five years the Iditarod had to start elsewhere.

"We used to have good, normal Alaskan winters here with tons of snow," Palin said. "But the last few years, nothing. It's empty, lonely, and bare."

Global warming was increasingly making headlines as weather patterns warmed and storms grew more severe worldwide. A growing body of scientific evidence reinforced expert claims about pending disaster. Palin was a leader in one of the nation's top oil-producing states, one that depends on the extraction industry. She acknowledged that global warming was occurring, but she would continue to argue against experts that warming was being accelerated by man-made causes such as pollution from the burning of fossil fuels—like oil.

After her first year on the job she took credit for engineering the city's growth, for developing its airport, extending access roads, water, and sewer line expansion, and drawing new businesses. Such civic feats can't be done in one lone year. Big projects take years to get from the drawing board to being ready to open for business. So credit technically was also due to her predecessor in the mayor's office, though she didn't say that. Palin's timing was perfect—she was the one in charge when so many doors opened for business in town.

In the 1999 mayoral race, Palin ran against the man she defeated for the job, her one-time friend John Stein. The *Frontiersman* newspaper called their race a struggle for political dominance in the region.

Palin campaigned for less government, while at the same time she advocated that the government take more conservative stands on social issues. She had overwhelming support from the many special interest groups she had smartly courted and kept happy over the years.

Stein stood for more careful planning and land-use regulations to keep the city's exploding growth from getting out of control. He talked of government needing to improve the quality of life, not the quantity. He insisted, as he had in his last losing campaign, that social issues like gun control and abortion didn't matter in a local city race.

Ironically, in this election it was Stein who was arguing that the current mayor was a tax-and-spend politician. He noted that despite all her talk of cutting spending, under Mayor Palin, city hall salary costs had grown by more than a half-million dollars and the city's debt had skyrocketed.

None of his arguments were enough to stop Palin's charisma, her forceful and popular stands, and her strong political groundwork. She won reelection as Wasilla mayor by a landslide, 826-255, receiving more than 76 percent of votes cast. Her biggest critics, former friends Stein and Carney, were so defeated that eventually they moved out of town and Alaska altogether. And, the Palins kept up their winning ways. Todd took his second Iron Dog title in the winter of 2000.

The couple also built a large new lakefront home worth more than a half-million dollars, complete with a dock for Todd's Piper seaplane. While Todd did a lot of the construction work himself, there would remain questions: were the people who supplied free and reduced-cost goods and services really trying to buy influence with Palin, who was clearly a rising star in the state Republican Party? One of the building companies who helped the Palins financially also sponsored Todd's snowmobile racing team. The company later paid Sarah to make a TV commercial for them. And the same company that helped the Palins build their dream house would soon win the lucrative city contract to build the biggest project in Wasilla history, its $14.7 million sports complex and ice rink.

In her second term as mayor, Palin was determined to win even bigger prizes for her city, and beef up her political record. Although she had pledged to limit government spending, she proposed having the city spend $38,000 to hire a lobbyist in Washington, D.C. Palin's choice was a

Republican Party operative with strong political connections, a former aide to the powerful veteran U.S. senator Ted Stevens. Stevens ran the Senate Appropriations Committee, which doled out federal tax money and has often been referred to as the congressional piggy bank. The lobbyist steered $27 million in federal tax dollars to Wasilla. That was a staggering amount of money for a remote city of only 5,500 residents. Among the projects the federal government bought the city: a $1.9 million bus station, $90,000 in utility repairs, $15 million for a railroad project, $1 million for a communications center, and expansion of a highway from two to four lanes.

So many federal tax dollars were pouring into little Wasilla that it caught the attention of Senator John McCain. He was a veteran Republican from the western state of Arizona, and he was a strong supporter of ethical reform. Part of his reform agenda was trying to stop the wasting of federal money on "pork-barrel" earmarks like those that Mayor Palin's town was winning. Earmarks are a controversial but age-old practice. Whenever Congress has a major bill that involves federal spending, politicians attach their favored projects

to the bill, even if those pet projects have nothing to do with the bill being passed.

Earmarking proved to be good for Wasilla, but Senator McCain and good-government groups charged that they were bad for America as a whole. Everybody loses because such hogging of the resources compounds federal debt for everyone, according to the reformists' argument. Though he had never met Wasilla's Mayor Palin, McCain publicly assailed her earmarks as perfect examples of what was wrong with the system. The earmark controversy is something that would dog her on the race for the White House.

Another controversy that would shadow Palin's political career involved sex crimes. Alaska suffered from one of the highest rates of rape and sex crimes in the nation. In May 2000, Alaska's democratic governor signed a law preventing cities like Wasilla from charging victims of rape the cost of investigating the crime. Palin's new police chief publicly criticized the governor's new law, saying unless rape victims paid, it posed an unfair burden on taxpayers. Palin was silent on her city's practice of charging rape victims for police investigations into their attacks.

Alaska's governor Tony Knowles responded to criticism from people like Wasilla's chief by saying: "We would never bill the victim of a burglary for fingerprinting and photographing a crime scene or for the cost of gathering other evidence. Nor should we bill rape victims just because the crime scene happens to be their bodies."

During her second term as mayor, Palin gave birth to her fourth child on March 2001. Like all the Palin children, the newborn's name reflected Todd and Sarah's Alaskan identity. They named her Piper, after the manufacturer of her father's seaplane.

Palin's biggest accomplishment as mayor was the sports complex she had proposed to keep youth focused on positive activities. The region was suffering from a rising drug and petty-crime problem. There were roving bands of homeless youths living in the local woods, because big city problems had come to roost in the growing valley.

Some townspeople were still pushing for the city to invest in a new library instead. With Palin's urging the sports complex won out. The complex final price tag was $14.7 million. The complex provided indoor basketball, soccer, and an Olympic-sized ice rink. The rink was important in a state obsessed with ice hockey. Palin's kids were active in all kinds of sports, especially hockey. Her son was a star and she would often make jokes about the legendary determination of hockey mothers to get their sons ahead in the fiercely competitive sport.

To pay for the project she saw as her legacy, Palin proposed the city borrow the funds via municipal bonds, which required taxpayers to pay back the funds plus interest by raising the sales tax by a half-percent. Palin started her political career backing the city's 2 percent sales tax, and the sports complex added another half-cent to the tax burden. Nobody likes to pay taxes, and conservatives who made up the majority of Palin's backers generally oppose increased government spending. The vote was close: 306-286. But Palin had skillfully convinced townspeople that progress does have a price.

So determined was Palin to get the complex launched while she was in office she may have rushed the deal. The city started construction before it even owned the land. It would take months of expensive legal wrangling, costing more than one million dollars extra on the projects. The messy closing details didn't get settled until long after Palin left office.

Chapter **6**

Big Time

In November 2001, after her mayoral term expired, the thirty-eight-year-old Palin faced a winter of unemployment. Then she got a call from the powerful Republican senator Frank Murkowski. He was leaving his seat as Alaska's member in the U.S. Senate to run for governor. He asked Palin to run to become his lieutenant governor. Although she was not the only Republican running for the post, it was a huge honor to get his backing.

Palin knew from experience that to fulfill her ambitions she would need mentors to help her climb the next rung. Mentors had helped her rise from housewife to career politician, and from tomboy to beauty queen. She had many Republican contacts she had been courting for years to turn to.

Strategically, to win higher office, she needed to appeal not just to her conservative local supporters who voted her into the Wasilla mayor's office, but to all Alaskans. To do that she got a political makeover that included leaving her longtime church. The pastor of Wasilla's Assembly of God had drawn controversy with some of his views, including telling supporters of a democratic presidential nominee that they would never get into heaven. She switched to the more sedate Wasilla Bible Church, a non-denominational Christian church where parishioners don't talk in tongues and were less likely to scare off mainstream voters.

Todd and Palin also severed connections to the controversial Alaska Independence Party (AIP), a political party that the media considered a fringe separatist group. The AIP advocated splitting off from

Frank Murkowski

the United States and declaring Alaska a sovereign nation. The group gained attention when former Republican governor Walter Hickel was elected governor in 1990 on the AIP ticket. Hickel soon returned to the Republican Party, and would become an important supporter for Palin—support he would later reverse.

Palin and Todd had attended the Alaskan Independence Party's statewide convention in 1994 in Wasilla. Todd joined the party in 1995 and would remain a member for all but two months of the next seven years. Palin spoke to the separatist group in 2006 during her campaign for governor. And she delivered a videotaped speech to the party convention in 2008. The Palins' involvement would become an issue as Palin sought higher office.

Before she could face all of Alaska's voters she would have to win the approval of the state's Republicans in a partisan primary election—a political semifinals. There were five Republican candidates, with Palin being the youngest and least experienced. But as her challengers always learned, it is unwise to underestimate Palin.

Palin's growing collection of powerful friends in the GOP helped her in her first bid for state office. They marketed her as a fresh face, with fresh ideas. She sought support from some of the most powerful figures in the state in the oil industry. Oil is one of the world's most sought-after resources and Alaska's biggest industry. Among the political contributions she took from the oil industry was a sizable donation from VECO, an oil company that soon would became part of a major bribery scandal.

Her main opponent had four times the money she had to spend on commercials and campaigning. Again Palin relied instead on one of her best assets, her charisma. She went everywhere, marching in parades and speaking to groups large and small. Todd spent entire days driving hundreds of miles at a time across Alaska to post campaign signs. With the help of family he took care of their children, aged one to thirteen years old.

Palin was still Wasilla's mayor while her lieutenant-governor campaign was caught in a crucial mistake. She and her campaign were cited for using Wasilla City Hall for political activities, which is illegal.

In her first statewide race she got her first lesson in being on the receiving end of hardball politics. A last-minute political propaganda piece made negative headlines by slamming her 1993 fishing violation—the one that had been entered mistakenly as a felony. And though she clarified the issue to the media, it was hard to erase the negative impression of her as a lawbreaker. Palin lost the primary election on August 28, 2002. But the race had proved far closer than predicted, and her surprise strong showing by coming in second put her on the political map.

She was clearly a rising star politically and people were starting to pay attention. Her secret was her ability to connect to regular people, said Steve Haycock, a history professor at the University of Alaska. "She is bright and has unfailing political instincts. She taps very directly into anxieties about the economic future."

Back home after her loss, Palin faced an uncomfortable situation. Since Palin was blocked by term limits for running for mayor again, the seat was wide open. Her friend was running to replace her in office. But so was Todd's stepmother, Faye Palin. Sarah Palin pointedly did not endorse her own mother-in-law. Faye was a Democrat and held more liberal social views than Sarah. When it was rumored that Faye was pro-choice on abortion rights, her campaign signs were defaced with spray-painted accusations that she was a "baby killer." She lost the election.

Palin had not given up her dreams for the political big time. Her next challenge was trying to get appointed by the outgoing Senator Murkowski; after all, she had worked hard for his successful campaign to become Alaska's governor. Her new political patron would be naming his own replacement to fill his now-vacant seat in the U.S. Senate.

In the end, however, Alaska's new governor appointed his own daughter, Lisa Murkowski, to replace him in the Senate. An attorney and a moderate Republican already in the state House of Representatives, Lisa Murkowski was more experienced and educated than Sarah. Still, Palin felt betrayed.

Alaska's new governor did not abandon Palin. He offered her a lucrative post as head of the Alaska Oil and Gas Conservation Commission, at a $125,000 salary. The commission is a three-member independent group that oversees the state's oil and gas industry. It was an industry Sarah knew nothing about, and she was now head of a staff of two dozen engineers, geologists, petroleum inspectors, and professionals whose duties also included safeguarding the environment against damage from the oil companies. The governor also appointed to the commission the state Republican Party chairman and prominent fundraiser, Randy Ruedrich. Ruedrich had the technical background for the job, because he held a PhD in chemical engineering and had thirty years' experience in the oil industry.

Palin's powerful new commissioner job also included serving as the ethics supervisor. She was distressed that Ruedrich did not resign his political post when he took the job. She felt it was wrong to be serving as the public's watchdog while still serving another master, in this case partisan politics. Still, Alaska's state legislature confirmed Ruedrich without requiring his resignation from the partisan political job.

Palin worked hard learning the technical information needed to do her job capably, with the help of the Oil Commission staff. As she performed her duties she became alarmed that her fellow commissioner, Ruedrich, was mixing his political business with the commission business. She believed his public appearances on behalf of private enterprise gave the bad appearance that there was no difference between the state of Alaska and the Republican Party. She found it not only morally wrong, but also illegal. As chairman and head of ethics, she worried that she would be blamed for the lapses.

She quietly turned to friends in the Republican Party for help behind the scenes. But after months went by and nothing changed, she was concerned her complaints were being ignored. So she went public with her accusations. She called for the resignation of Reudrich, but he refused. Despite all her ambitions and the financial benefits of the job, Palin felt she needed to keep her integrity intact. She resigned from the Oil and Gas Commission in 2004. In the end, Ruedrich was forced to resign and pay

The Trans-Alaska Pipeline under the midnight sun on the North Slope

$12,000 in fines, the largest of its kind in state history. He kept his position as head of the state's Republican Party.

Back home, she threw herself back into the world of family, volunteering, and making up for lost time as a hockey mom. Her time as a stay-at-home mom ended on October 18, 2005. The date had much significance. It was Alaska Day, a statewide holiday commemorating the Alaskan Territory being formally transferred from Russia ownership in 1867 to the United States. It was also daughter Bristol's birthday. Palin threw a big party to celebrate daughter Bristol turning fifteen. At the party Palin made her public announcement that she was running for governor.

Political experts dismissed her as a long-shot candidate against the powerful Republican governor Murkowski, who had spent six terms as a U.S. senator. Politically, he appeared entrenched and insurmountable. Personally, he was the man who put her on the map politically. Here was another mentor she would need to climb over to fulfill her ambitions. But she felt his handling of the office lacked integrity.

Her long-shot campaign started without even an office, with Palin working out of the back of her car. Instead of a business-like briefcase she toted things in a basket. But her reputation had grown as a good-government reformer, and she drew a lot of hard-working early supporters from people impressed with her principled stand at the Oil and Gas Commission. She also got lucky with her timing. Scandal erupted.

News of a broad criminal conspiracy investigation shocked the state. Powerful men involved in the oil business and state legislators were having their offices raided by federal authorities. For months the wide-ranging probe would spill out more ugly scandals and land many of the most powerful men in the nation in jail. Bribery, conspiracy, kickbacks: the headlines exposed it all.

Governor Murkowski was no longer as insurmountable as Alaska's Mount McKinley. His

The Alaska State Capitol building

popularity in polls dropped as low as 15 percent before the primary election.

Meanwhile, as his fortunes sank, Palin's rose. Her grassroots campaign had snowballed as she made the most of her "Mrs.

Palin and her husband Todd during a fundraiser in Anchorage, Alaska

Clean" reputation and folksy style. She made TV commercials with five-year-old Piper on her hip, and another jogging alongside teenage Bristol. People liked what they saw. She won the Republican primary with 51 percent of vote. The once mighty Murkowski took only 19 percent.

The GOP was facing corruption accusations not just in Alaska, but in other parts of the nation and in Washington, D.C., in the Republican administration of President George W. Bush, a former oilman himself. Ethics became the big word, one that challenged the Democrats as well. The Republican Party desperately needed to prove it had some. Palin seemed made to order, but the party bosses refused to see her appeal and back her. However, the voters did and volunteers flocked to her campaign.

In her personal life Palin faced a tough decision. Her first child, Track, was a star ice hockey player and was entering his senior year in high school. The family discussed how to handle his looming adulthood and his reputation as a party boy. A Michigan family whose son also was a serious hockey player offered to let Track live with them and attend school there. This plan meant that their child would be nearly 4,000 miles away. The Palins decided that in the Midwest Track would get better exposure to scouts for college and professional ice hockey teams. So their firstborn spent most of his last year of high school away from home.

In Alaska's November 2006 general election, Palin ran against Democrat Anthony "Tony" Knowles, a former state representative and two-term Alaska governor. The race featured a third independent-party candidate, Andrew Halcro, a businessman and two-term Republican state legislator. The two men felt their best strategy would be to debate Palin as often as they could—as many as twenty-five debates throughout the state—to highlight what they felt was her superficial knowledge of the issues and her extreme conservative positions on social issues.

Their strategy backfired. Staging more debates gave Palin more time on stage, where she loved to be. She relied on her charm and spoke in generalities instead of getting tripped up in facts and figures. Her performances frustrated Halcro, who felt like Palin was the kind of person who never did her homework in school and yet always got better grades than he did.

Said Halcro, "Palin is a master of the nonanswer. She can turn a 60-second response to a query about her specific solutions to healthcare challenges into a folksy story about how she's met people on the campaign trail who face health care challenges. All without uttering a word about her public-policy solutions to health care challenges."

Palin talked to her opponent about their differences and he never forgot the way she summed up her appeal: "Andrew, I watch you at these debates with no notes, no papers, and yet when asked questions, you spout off facts, figures, and policies, and I'm amazed. But then I look out into the audience and I ask myself, 'Does any of this really matter?'" Palin said.

Alaskans wanted a reprieve from the unrelenting scandals filling their daily newspapers. Palin presented herself as the clean, fresh snow—unmuddied by corruption. On the one hand the state power brokers publicly dismissed her as a lightweight but privately they threw their weight into taking her down.

"Anyone who was part of the Establishment fought against her. [Prominent news personality] Dan Fagan clawed, fought, ridiculed, embarrassed and deliberately misrepresented Sarah," said Frank Bailey, a stay-at-home dad who became one of her first and most committed volunteers.

Palin did face some hard questions during the race. She was questioned on whether her personal evangelical Christian beliefs would interfere with her governing. Palin never tried to keep her religious beliefs secret. She acknowledged during the campaign that she believed in the biblical view of how the world began, that it was created by God in seven days, compared to the scientific theory that life evolved on Earth over millions of years. She openly backed the controversial notion that the Christian life-origin belief of creationism should be taught in schools alongside the scientific evolution facts.

"I am a proponent of teaching both. And you know, I say this too as the daughter of a science teacher. Growing up with being so privileged and blessed to be given a lot of information on, on both sides of the subject—creationism and evolution. It's been a healthy foundation for me," she said.

Alaska is hard to predict politically. More than half of its 465,000 registered voters are Independents. Registered Republicans outnumber Democrats 2-to-1. Independents came through for Palin. She won the race with 48 percent of the vote, while the former Democratic governor took 41 percent, and the independent candidate Halcro 9 percent.

Her win followed the hard-won equality gains of political pioneering women who had come before her. America first considered Alaska's purchase a mistake when Russia sold it in the 1860s. Then after the gold rush its precious resources commanded more respect from America when it was promoted to the status of full-fledged U.S. territory in 1912. That came at a time when American women were still fighting for the right to vote.

Women had made great strides in equality by the time Palin started shining in the world of high school athletics. She was able to compete athletically because of the recent gains of Title 9, the 1972 federal statute that guaranteed that in public education girls had the same rights and share of the budget as boys. By gaining these toe holds in equal rights, women continued climbing to the top. The first woman governor elected in her own right was Ella Grasso of Connecticut. Thirty-two years later, Sarah Palin became governor of Alaska.

She couldn't have timed it more perfectly. Palin had the good fortune to be inaugurated fifty years after Alaska became the forty-ninth state. Her master of ceremonies was one of her heroes, Libby Riddles, the first woman to win the Iditarod sled-dog race. Palin thanked Riddles, saying, "She was bold and tough. Thank you for paving the way."

Palin herself had proved that she too was bold and tough and paving the way. She became the first woman governor and the youngest in that state's nearly half-century history. She would be running America's largest state, in land area, for only a short time before another major first would come her way.

Women United for Palin shout out to passing traffic during a demonstration in Anchorage, Alaska.

Chapter 7

Governor Sarah

S arah Palin's inaugural speech was ambitious in scope, showing that the new governor was looking far beyond Alaska's big borders.

"America is looking for answers," she said. "She is looking for a new direction, the world is looking for a new light. . . . That light came from America's great north star. It can come from Alaska."

Though the Palin family moved into the stately Governor's Mansion, she maintained her folksy relationship with the voters so much that most people referred to her as Governor Sarah or simply Sarah. Todd was dubbed "The First Dude." It was a funny and hip twist on the custom of the spouse of a president, prime minister, or governor being called "The First Lady," since most top leaders have been men historically.

Soon afterward Todd went on to capture his fourth Iron Dog title. The Palins were continuing their winning streak.

Her campaign had included debate about hot-button social issues like gun control and abortion. She had said publicly she would oppose abortion even if her own daughter had been impregnated by a rapist. But most of her campaign emphasized the meatier issues of the state's business—resource development like oil and natural gas, crime, education, and jobs.

As governor, Palin bolted out of the starting gate with sweeping changes, cleaning up the way Alaska did business. She made great political fanfare out of her handling of one of the biggest symbols of the excesses of the previous administration, selling the former governor's $2.7-million jet.

She made bold moves to police the oil industry more strictly, increased oil taxes, and opened the industry up to more competitive bidding to try and end the monopoly of the biggest companies. It takes steely determination to take on the oil companies—the industry accounts for 85 percent of the state's annual tax revenue, and because of this oil wealth, the state's residents pay no income tax. In addition, every resident gets an annual rebate of oil profits from the state's Permanent Fund.

Palin's timing as always was perfect; rising oil prices globally meant bigger profits shared locally by Alaskans. In Palin's first year in office the fund provided $3,000 per resident, almost twice what they received the year before. It helped her popularity that a typical family of four received $12,000 from Governor Sarah.

Palin rebuilt good relations with the state legislature, Republicans and Democrats alike. She engineered the framework to install a billion-dollar natural-gas pipeline to ease the exportation and earn more money for the state developing this precious natural resource. The pipeline she believed would be her biggest legacy.

Legislatively she kept a division between church and state. She vetoed legislation that would have killed health benefits to workers in gay relationships, despite the evangelical Christian belief that homosexuality is sinful. She followed her pledge to not push her belief in biblical creationism into the state educational system.

Palin's unaffected manner and casual dress connected with voters. She wasn't entirely unconcerned about her good looks, however. She continued running to stay trim, and spent thousands of dollars of her own money installing a tanning bed in the Governor's Mansion.

Alaskans liked that she did not come from an elite and sophisticated background. She had never traveled much, and she got her first passport in 2007 in order to visit Alaskan National Guard troops in Kuwait on their way to the Iraq war.

She registered an astounding 90 percent approval rating in the polls. Still, she was criticized for giving several highly placed political jobs to personal friends from high school and her church, some of whom had little or no experience or qualifications. One such appointment went to an ex-real estate agent who cited her childhood love of cows as a qualification for the $95,000-a-year job as director of the State Agriculture Department.

State of Alaska Governor's Mansion

Another sticky issue that hurt Palin's image was one very expensive bridge.

While campaigning for governor in 2006, she had visited the rural town of Ketchikan near where she had spent her early childhood. There she spoke in favor of an issue important to the townspeople, a proposed bridge linking the town to the local airport on Gravina Island, which had a population of only about fifty people. The $400-million bridge project was funded by a congressional earmark secured by the powerful U.S. senator Ted Stevens and Alaska's sole congressman Don Young, both Republicans.

Opponents of earmarking seized on the Gravina Island bridge as a prime example of government waste, and nicknamed the project "The Bridge to Nowhere." Then later as governor, Palin reversed her support. She halted state work on the bridge project in September 2007 amid a national furor over congressional earmarking and government waste. Still later she would take credit for personally stepping in to stand up to government waste, in fact using it as a testament to her strong ethical backbone. "I told the Congress, 'Thanks, but no thanks,' on that Bridge to Nowhere."

However, when voters looked past the catchy slogan, they found that Governor Palin cancelled the bridge but kept the $400 million in federal earmarks for other state transportation projects. Critics claimed it was as if she took out a public library book, then kept it for her own, while claiming she deserved praise for refusing to take the library book.

Under Palin, the state invested billions of dollars in infrastructure, revamped the educational funding system, and restored a senior citizens program to help low-income elderly, a program that Murkowski had cut. She also created Alaska's Petroleum Systems Integrity Office to ensure oil and gas extraction equipment was working properly to avoid spillage and pollution.

She still advocated that humans had nothing to do with global warming, but she recognized the experts and the obvious signs that global warming was causing disastrous problems in Alaska. She created a committee to prepare a climate change strategy for Alaska.

Nearly a year after she took office, Palin's son Track, who had turned eighteen, enlisted in the Army on September 11, 2007—the anniversary of the terrorist attacks on America. Then Palin became pregnant with her fifth child, which she kept secret from most of her family and staff until near the end of her pregnancy. When she announced her pregnancy at seven months, she said, "To any critics who say a woman can't think and work and carry a baby at the same time I'd like to just escort that Neanderthal back to the cave."

There was an even deeper secret about her pregnancy that she revealed to no one but Todd.

As she neared the end of her pregnancy in April 2008 she flew to Texas for the Republican Governors Association meeting. Medical experts advise against flying past the thirty-sixth week of pregnancy because airplane cabin pressure can cause problems, but Palin was determined.

Before dawn in her hotel room, she went into premature labor. Palin was set to give one of the highlighted speeches later in the day, and she delivered the speech despite her secret endurance of labor contractions. Palin flew back to Alaska, where Todd met her at the airport and drove back to Wasilla. Some eight hours after landing back home, she delivered the baby.

The Tongass Narrows separates Ketchikan from the airport on Gravina Island as seen in this December 16, 2005, photograph. Ferry service provides transportation between the two sides.

Her son Trig was born with Down syndrome, a genetic disorder that limits mental and physical abilities, sometimes severely. His parents named him for the Norse word for "brave victory" and "true." She returned to work in the governor's office three days after giving birth to her special needs baby. Todd took a leave of absence from his oil-production job to help care for the family.

Doctors had told her early in the pregnancy of his disability, but she said she never had any doubts about whether to terminate the pregnancy because of his Down syndrome.

As she privately wrestled with the emotions about what it would mean to care for a disabled child, she wrote an e-mail letter to her family introducing the newest Palin: "This new person in your life can help put things in perspective and bind us together and get everyone focused on what really matters . . . those who love him will think less about self and focus less on what the world tells us is 'normal and perfect.' "

Palin didn't sign the e-mail letter with her name. Instead she showed the depths of the spiritual side of her reasoning. She signed it in the name of God, as "Trig's creator, Your Heavenly Father."

Palin had her hands more than full as the ultimate working wife and mother, with five children, and her job as governor. But she wanted more.

She worked to increase her national profile, spending $31,000 of state money for a publicist. She argued to the state legislature that it would help Alaska to have Palin appear as a spokesperson for gas and oil issues and promote the proposed natural-gas pipeline.

In February 2008 she traveled to Washington, D.C., for the National Governors' Conference, where she met with Senator

John McCain, who was making another run for president on the Republican ticket. He told her she was on his list of possible vice-presidential candidates to run with him.

Back home, turmoil in Palin's family life began negatively impacting her public profile. While she was running for lieutenant governor and governor, Palin's sister, Molly McCann, was going through marital problems with her second husband, Mike Wooten. Wooten was a thirty-two-year-old Alaska state trooper and former Air Force veteran. The couple had four children, two of them hers from a first marriage.

Wooten had been disciplined by the state troopers for several transgressions, including unsafe driving. He also used his Taser stun gun on his own eleven-year-old stepson, because the boy wanted to show off to his cousin, Bristol Palin, how tough he was. Palin's sister Molly later reported her estranged husband for illegally killing a moose without a permit, while she was hunting with him and carried a permit in her name. When officials learned of his illegal kill, he was relieved from duty as wildlife investigator.

Molly went to court to get a domestic-violence restraining order against him and filed for divorce in April 2005. The result of these complaints was that Wooten was suspended from the force and received other official reprimands. However, the Palin family felt he deserved more severe punishment. The Palin family was so worried about Wooten they hired a private investigator. Behind the scenes the Palin family and associates had pushed for Wooten to be fired altogether. The extent of their maneuvering would be the subject of much speculation and official investigation in the months to come. Palin wrote a letter to state officials complaining the force was not being active enough to take action against Wooten, who she characterized as "a ticking time bomb."

Troopergate, as it came to be known, reached boiling point on July 11, 2008, when Governor Palin fired the man she had named as head of the Alaska state troopers, Alaska public safety commissioner Walt Monegan. Her official reason for firing him was insubordination and failure to follow her fiscal reforms. However, despite the finding that he was an unfit employee, she offered him another state job with a slightly lower salary.

Monegan refused the job and went public with the firing. He told the media he believed he was terminated because he stood up to considerable pressure from the Palin camp for refusing to fire Wooten from the force. The firing looked like personal revenge, instead of official legal business.

The story became national as speculation grew that Palin was on the list of possible running mates for Senator McCain's presidential run. Monegan's records showed that the Palin family and associates had contacted his office about firing Trooper Wooten more than two dozen times over a nineteen-month period. When Palin refused to backtrack or apologize despite legal advice to do so, in late July 2008 the state legislature launched an investigation.

The media reacted on the theory that where there's smoke, there's

Walt Monegan

fire. They started digging into Palin administration records more deeply, especially her travel and expense records. What they found made headlines: Palin had traveled extensively with her family on the taxpayers' expense, including trips to New York and to watch Todd compete in snowmobile races.

In her defense, the governor's office noted that they believed there was an expectation that Palin's family participate in community activities. Alaska authorities started talking about launching investigations.

Then the Troopergate controversy took another strange turn. After she fired the head of the state police, Walt Monegan, she replaced him with a lawman that had less experience but strong backing among evangelical Christians. Less than two weeks later, however, her new director of public safety, Chuck Kopp, was forced to resign. It became public that he had been officially reprimanded at his former job for sexually harassing an employee. Palin's mistake was politically damaging.

Palin also lost support by failing to protect an important symbol of Alaska, the polar bear. During her term as governor, the federal government listed polar bears as threatened with extinction. The government put the species under the protection of the federal Endangered Species Act. Alaska is home to an estimated one-fifth of the world's surviving 25,000 polar bears. But in Alaska and elsewhere the bear population is dangerously dwindling due to alarming levels of melting tundra that serves as their habitat and hunting grounds. Palin sued Republican president George Bush's administration demanding that the polar bear be freed from federal protection. Listing them, Palin's federal lawsuit maintained, would threaten the state's oil and gas industry more than it would hurt the bears.

Chapter **8**

Her Own Way

B y August 27, 2008, John McCain was about to be named the Republican Party nominee for president. And he wanted to talk to Palin about being his running mate.

On that day, McCain's campaign flew Palin on an unmarked private jet to Arizona where she was interviewed at length by the McCain campaign's top officials. Whether she would pass the test or get the nod she did not know. Already she was told the campaign had dug through her background. And, she could tell no one. The McCain campaign did not want the press to find out and ruin the advantage it would hold by making the announcement of a running mate in its own way.

Palin landed in Arizona and was taken where the press would never find them, at the private home of the chief executive of the liquor distribution company started by McCain's father-in-law. The campaign had only days to decide before the Republican Party nominating convention would begin.

Politically, McCain was falling behind the charismatic Democratic nominee Barack Obama. The Illinois senator was a law professor who had just made history as the first African American to win his party's nomination for president. He was drawing dramatic support from voters of all races and political ideology with his inspirational message, his clear intelligence, and his personal background of having overcome adversity to rise to the top levels of power.

McCain's advisers knew they needed a jolt of energy to get ahead of Obama. Voters worried about McCain's age; at seventy-two he would be the oldest first-term president ever. He faced concerns about his sometimes sharp temper, his shifting viewpoints, and his health challenges. He had battled skin cancer and had spent five torturous years as a Vietnamese prisoner of war. Palin was forty-four. She offered the ticket what McCain was lacking: youth, a common person's touch, and solid credentials with the Republican Party's key evangelical Christian supporters. Philosophically they had much in common in their goal for government reform and stronger ethics laws.

After interviewing Palin, McCain's strategists debated long into the night. Neither McCain nor the voters knew Palin; she was a gamble. McCain's top people, both men, thought she especially would appeal to women voters, and might even draw support from Democrats upset that New York senator Hillary

Palin acknowledges supporters as Republican presidential candidate Senator John McCain introduces her as his vice-presidential running mate.

Clinton, the former First Lady, had not been chosen as the Democratic nominee for president at the Democratic Convention earlier in the week.

McCain's strategist wondered: should they go with Connecticut senator Joe Lieberman? He was a Democratic candidate for vice president in 2000, but in 2006 he was elected to a fourth term as an Independent. Personally and professionally close to McCain, Lieberman as a running mate would have certainly made headlines as the experienced and bipartisan candidate. But Lieberman, who was Jewish, was staunchly for abortion rights and for equal rights for gays. Both positions would have dashed the already weak support for McCain carried among the conservative Christian voting bloc, one of the most important and motivated special interest groups in the nation.

On the plus side for Palin, her folksy charm and personal story about rising from modest means would serve as a healthy counter to his image as an out-of-touch member of America's wealthy elite. McCain was divorced and his second wife, Cindy, was an heiress. He had just caused a public furor by admitting he couldn't remember how many houses he had. (He owned six.) The nation was facing the worst economic meltdown since the Great Depression, and his strategists knew they needed someone who could relate to Walmart budget shoppers and let them know that the Republican Party understood their pain.

Palin passed the first test. Next they flew her to meet McCain at his vacation home in Sedona, a resort town in the high desert of northern Arizona. The pair talked at length and then walked by a creek, where McCain had Palin meet with Cindy McCain, to get his wife's opinion. Privately he asked his strategists for their final advice and they told him: she's high risk, but high reward. McCain was a former fighter pilot known in his military days for his cockiness, and throughout his life he believed in being a risk taker. He decided to take the risk on Sarah Palin.

She was whisked by the campaign in secret to Dayton, Ohio. It was an industrial town in a state where factories and farming had been crippled by the current economic meltdown, by international trade imbalances, and by outsourcing of jobs to lower-cost Third World countries.

On Thursday the Democrats had made history by officially naming Barack Obama as their nominee, making him the first African American major-party candidate for the White House. On Friday, August 29, 2008, McCain stole their thunder—and their TV cameras—when he announced that he had chosen as a running mate the first Republican woman candidate for vice president.

McCain introduced Palin as a new kind of leader. "It's with great pride and . . . that I tell you I have found the right partner to help me stand up to those who value their privileges over their responsibilities, who put power over principle."

Palin's first speech by the McCain campaign was written to immediately appeal to women. It was full of humble praise for the feminist trailblazers who had made her own rise into the top tier of politics possible. Even though it had been the Democrats who had broken the gender barrier decades ago, she graciously praised the first woman on a presidential ticket, Geraldine Ferraro. Ferraro was an ex-prosecuting attorney and New York politician who ran for vice president in 1984. She was the first to break the so-called glass ceiling that seemed to keep women from breaking into the top floors of power. Then Palin praised Hillary Clinton's achievements—the senator had come very close to becoming the first woman nominee for president of the United States.

Supporters hold signs up as Republican vice-presidential candidate Governor Sarah Palin enters the T. R. Hughes Ballpark in O'Fallon, Missouri, for a rally on August 31, 2008.

"Hillary left 18 million cracks in the highest, hardest glass ceiling in America, but it turns out the women of America aren't finished yet, and we can shatter that glass ceiling once and for all," Palin told the rally of 15,000 supporters.

Reporters and political operatives flooded to Alaska to find out about Palin, since her slender record was virtually unknown outside. McCain's staff was so unprepared for the frenzied interest in Palin some spokespeople weren't sure how to even pronounce her name. Alaska is a place so remote it has its own time zone. And, it is exotic to many Americans, whose hunt for food takes them to the abundantly filled grocery store instead of the hard-scrabble frontier where Palin grew up.

After the announcement Palin came forward with a deeply personal family matter she realized that the national media would soon discover: her unwed teenage daughter Bristol was five months pregnant.

Quickly McCain neutralized what could have been a major negative for a political party whose many backers considered premarital sex a sin. The pregnancy of seventeen-year-old Bristol might be considered shocking by some, especially because of the family's carefully constructed image as following a strict Christian wholesome lifestyle. McCain asked that the public respect the Palin family's privacy, and that to remember everyone, including teenagers, is human. The family released a statement saying that Bristol and her long-time boyfriend Levi Johnston would be married as soon as she turned eighteen and could legally do so. Later, however, after the campaign ended and only months after their baby boy, Tripp Johnston, was born, Levi would go public with unsavory statements about the Palin family, who he claimed pressured Bristol to break off their engagement.

The Obama campaign leaders reacted with shock at McCain's choice for running mate. They at first dismissed Palin as a "nobody" tarred with the growing Troopergate scandal.

Palin was being kept under wraps; other than campaign events she was kept from the press and public. But public curiosity about her reached fever pitch. Some 44 million people tuned in to hear what she had to say during her highly anticipated speech at the Republican National Convention in Minneapolis-St. Paul, the following week. And she delivered a fireworks display of a speech. She looked smart, folksy, and most of all, aggressive. Like a pit bull she attacked Obama and his gray-haired running mate Joe Biden with clever one-line zingers.

Palin also threw in humor, telling the joke that there was one difference between a hockey mom like her and a pit bull: lipstick. It was a joke and a warning rolled into one. Conventioneers reacted with wild applause, and Palin became an overnight sensation. The media called it Palin-mania.

Suddenly her name and picture seemed to appear everywhere and crowds swelled at campaign events. Within twenty-four hours, the McCain campaign raised $7 million in donations. Volunteers flooded in. Going into the Republican Convention, Obama had a six-point lead. By the end of the week, McCain was ahead by two points. Palin was a star, a political Cinderella story.

A week after the Convention, Palin flew home to Alaska to see her son Track deploy to fight in the Iraq war. The unpopular war was dragging into its sixth year with more than 5,000 military men and women killed there, tens of thousands more injured. The Bush administration had begun the war by invading Iraq, which was the first time in its history that America had launched an unprovoked attack on a sovereign nation. And, increasingly, Americans considered it a mistake that must end. Obama had won the Democratic nomination in part because of his early stand against the invasion and war. One of the starkest differences between the candidates McCain and Obama was their visions of how to handle the Iraq war, and how and when to end it. Palin had spoken about the war in a controversial manner, casting it in religious terms as "God's plan."

As Palin continued to campaign many were inspired by her story of being a self-made candidate with integrity. Others criticized her as too much style over substance. Most voters, however, were trying to keep an open mind and learn her views and political record first before they judged. Both political leaders and average voters alike questioned whether Palin had the qualifications to step into the shoes of leader of the free world.

Even prominent Republicans like Nebraska senator Chuck Hagel voiced doubts about her publicly, "She doesn't have any foreign policy credentials. . . . I think it's a stretch to, in any way, to say that she's got the experience to be President of the United States."

The Republican strategy was to keep highlighting Palin's appeal to women voters. In the case of many leaders of women's political groups, however, that strategy didn't wash. Prominent feminist Gloria Steinem argued that the only thing Sarah Palin had in common with real feminists was "the female chromosome." Feminism has never been about getting a job for one woman, argued Steinem who helped found the women's movement in the late twentieth century. "It's about making life more fair for women everywhere."

Even Palin's fellow Alaska Republican legislator Lyda Green of Wasilla slammed her. "She's not prepared to be governor. How can she be prepared to be vice president or president? Look at what she's done to this state. What would she do to the nation?," said Green, president of the Alaska state Senate.

None of this seemed to dim Palin's star power. Whether the media and voters loved or hated Palin, everyone seemed to want more of her. The McCain campaign was keeping her off limits. She gave no interviews and delivered only heavily scripted speeches, frustrating many people who felt they didn't have enough information to decide for themselves about her.

When the campaign did allow her to speak to the media, it was only to a handful of carefully selected interviewers in easy to control situations like one-on-one interviews. Even so, Palin stumbled on important details. And voters worried that anyone who sits a heartbeat away from the presidency should know details. She couldn't name more than one important Supreme Court decision. She didn't know the economic record of her running mate. She wasn't clear what exactly a vice president of the United States did.

At one point the McCain campaign claimed Palin did have foreign policy experience because Russia can be seen from Alaska. The statement caused enormous criticism; it was as if McCain's campaign was arguing that someone can be a math expert because they sit beside an algebra textbook.

Palin performed like a trooper despite the hardball treatment in the political big leagues. She always looked sharp, she always smiled, and she dressed in fashionable clothes tailored to fit her perfectly. She looked like a celebrity instead of a hockey mom. Then it leaked out that the campaign had spent more than $150,000 on her expensive makeovers and clothing from high-end stores. Her family too had been dressed and styled by the campaign. Damaging criticism was heaped on them that they were being phonies; the Palins claimed they represented Main Street America, when they were really closer to representing the Wall Street corporate elite. One newspaper writer dismissed Palin as Caribou Barbie, simply a pretty doll with a fantastic wardrobe but an empty plastic head.

It was clear Palin needed to do something impressive to get people to take her seriously. She and the campaign strategists worked hard to get her ready for the vice-presidential debate on October 2, 2008. On live national television she would match wits with Senator Joe Biden. The democratic vice-presidential candidate was an attorney and one of the longest-serving senators in history. He was smart, and he had extensive knowledge of legal issues and foreign policy. Plus his personal story appealed to many voters because Biden had overcome humble beginnings to climb to the pinnacle of power, as had his running mate Barack Obama.

Palin studied as if for the most important final examination of her life. She used color-coded note cards to learn the basics of world affairs and economic issues, to show how serious she really was.

At the debate, Palin zeroed in on her opponent with her personal charm from the start, as she asked the distinguished senator, "Can I call you Joe?"

Biden easily won the debate according to polls. But Palin received much praise for meeting the expectations analysts had set for her, even if those expectations were lower. During the debate she grew so confidant that she tried some of her trade-

mark folksy gestures. While the candidates spoke about deadly serious topics like war, global warming, and the suffering of the forty million Americans without health care, Palin took time to give saucy winks into the camera and give a shout-out to an elementary school class.

For some viewers Palin's performance was a knockout. One journalist wrote, "I'm sure I'm not the only male in America who, when Palin dropped her first wink, sat up a little straighter on

Palin and Joe Biden take part in the vice-presidential debate at Washington University in St. Louis, Missouri, October 2, 2008.

the couch and said, 'Hey, I think she just winked at me.' And her smile. By the end, when she clearly knew she was doing well, it was so sparkling it was almost mesmerizing. It sent little starbursts through the screen and ricocheting around the living rooms of America."

Most reviews were not so kind, however. They maintained that the debates were the first real test of what Sarah Palin really had to offer intellectually, and that she was lacking.

The heels are on, the gloves are off.

Sarah Palin

The Republican crowd still adored her, though. With the debate behind her, Palin seemed to regain her footing. She started relying on her own political instincts more and resisting the advice of McCain's campaign staff. She even publicly disagreed with her boss, the potential president of the United States.

Palin became even more aggressive with her criticism of her opponents. As she said, "The heels are on, the gloves are off."

She ridiculed Obama's early career as a nothing job. After graduating from a prestigious college, Obama sidetracked his career to work as a community organizer to help the disadvantaged in the poor neighborhoods of Chicago, Illinois.

She claimed Obama consorted with terrorists, because one of his professional associates had been an antiwar activist with a violent past during the Vietnam War era, thirty years before Obama knew him. Many voters criticized Palin for causing hysteria by unfairly connecting Obama to actions that had nothing to do with him. Her stinging criticism was turning off the majority of voters. After eight years of brutal partisan politics, Americans were growing tired of the politics of personal destruction. They wanted to hear about plans for the future.

Perhaps the biggest damage to Palin's political credentials came from an unusual source: the entertainment world. Writer

Tina Fey was an actress on a late-night TV show, *Saturday Night Live*, that was popular among young and educated viewers. Fey made fun of Palin by dressing up to look just like her, with her designer eyeglasses, her high heels, and her broad accent peppered with folksy "yups." Fey's version of the vice-presidential candidate presented her as a silly airhead. What made her satire most effective is that she often used Palin's own words to spoof her. Even voters who didn't follow the political race closely still couldn't miss these performances, which were funny five-minute skits people could get easily off the Internet.

While the spoofs of Palin made news and drew millions of viewers, not everyone was laughing. The caricatures damaged the McCain-Palin standing. Palin gamely tried to fight back by appearing on the network TV show herself, side-by-side with Fey; they even dressed in an identical outfit. It was gutsy for Palin to confront one of her most effective critics on live television, but it failed to erase the damage.

Obama and Biden kept rising higher in the polls while McCain-Palin sank. Internal disagreements that had been going on behind the scenes of the McCain campaign began to spill out in public. News stories revealed that campaign aides blamed Palin and her behavior for low poll numbers. They claimed she was so uninformed she thought Africa was a country not a continent, that she was a temperamental diva and not a disciplined political leader. Behind her back, aides called her "The Little Shop of Horrors."

Palin decided to defy McCain's losing campaign, and started doing things her way. But her actions only lead to even more acrimony: political pundits accused Palin of not following orders and "going rogue."

Three days before the election, McCain appeared on *Saturday Night Live.* Standing beside the Republican candidate, actress Tina Fey impersonated Palin. "Okay, listen up everybody, I am goin' rogue right now so keep your voices down," said Fey, spoofing Palin. "Available now, we got a buncha' these 'Palin in 2012' T-shirts. Just try and wait until after Tuesday (election day) to wear 'em okay? Because I'm not goin' anywhere. And I'm certainly not goin' back to Alaska. If I'm not goin' to the White House, I'm either runnin' in four years or I'm gonna be a white Oprah so, you know, I'm good either way."

Election 2008 drew the highest voter turnout in forty years, more than 130 million voters. Obama decisively won the Electoral College votes, which officially determine the election. And he won the popular vote, winning 52.9 percent compared to McCain-Palin with 45.7.

McCain gave a gracious concession speech at a historic hotel in his home state of Arizona. He praised President-elect Obama and spoke about how important his triumph over prejudice was to America.

"His success alone commands my respect for his ability and perseverance. But that he managed to do so by inspiring the hopes of so many millions of Americans who had once wrongly believed that they had little at stake or little influence in the election of an American president is something I deeply admire and commend him for achieving."

McCain thanked Palin in his speech, calling her one of the best campaigners he had ever seen: "An impressive new voice in our party for reform and the principles that have always been our greatest strength. . . . We can all look forward with great interest to her future service to Alaska, the Republican Party, and our country."

Palin tried to give a concession speech as well. She had one written but McCain aides refused to let her speak, explaining that this violated long-standing campaign tradition. Not satisfied, Palin appealed to the candidate himself to let her speak. McCain shot her down.

After the election, Palin returned home and to the job she had been elected to do—govern Alaska. She was barely halfway through her first term. But she was no longer beloved by Alaskans. Her poll numbers kept dropping. She was being swarmed with scandals and investigations small and large.

In an interview soon after the November 4 election, Palin confessed that political ambition still burned inside her despite her loss. "Don't let me miss the open door. Show me where the open door is and even if it's cracked up a little bit, maybe I'll just plow right on through that and maybe prematurely plow through it, but don't let me miss an open door. And if there is an open door in '12 or four years later, and if it is something that is going to be good for my family, for my state, for my nation, an opportunity for me, then I'll plow through that door."

She continued to prove her star-power, by remaining in the headlines beyond Alaska's borders.

Then she stunned supporters and foes alike when she resigned office on July 3, 2009, with a year and a half left to go in her term. Palin said she needed to protect her family, and that they had suffered under the spotlight. She said she needed to leave to escape the numerous investigations that have drained her financially and hurt her ability to govern. "I love my job and I love Alaska, and it hurts to make this choice, but I'm doing what's best for them," she said.

Three months before her surprise resignation, Palin signed a deal for an undisclosed sum to write her autobiography. And, after she quit her job as governor she left the state to write her book. Yet her following remained so strong that even without an official office to elevate her importance, she remained in the news headlines. She continued her public criticism of President Obama. She showed her populist appeal by inviting anyone who wanted to subscribe to her Internet sites to be able to read up on her musings, opinions, and sometimes just chatty news about her life and family.

Sarah Palin is credited with rejuvenating and reviving the image of the troubled Republican Party in Alaska. And she helped revive the image of the national Republican Party. She captured the hearts and attention of the most conservative wing of the national party.

"Her appeal to people in the party (and in the country) who share her convictions and resentments is profound. The fascination is viral, and global," wrote one journalist.

Her many critics argue that she lacks both the qualifications and the temperament to serve at the top levels of government. But people continue to either love or hate her. And, on one issue the majority agrees: she served as a role model for working mothers. She was the real-life Super Mom who held onto her values as she rose to the top.

Palin continues to stay in the spotlight and affect public debate. She has been called the new face of the Republican Party, and interest in her remains so high that a fan paid $63,500 to dine with her—the high-price dinner was a prize in an Internet charity auction to benefit wounded veterans.

And, defying expectations again, Palin wrote her highly anticipated memoir in four months' time. The 400-page book, titled *Going Rogue: An American Story*, was written in collaboration with Lynn Vincent, a San Diego-based writer and features editor for *World* magazine, a conservative Christian publication. Preorders pushed the book to number one on both Amazon.com and Barnes & Noble.com just two days after the announcement of its early release.

As prominent conservative Brent Bozell put it, "Conservatives have been looking for leadership, and [Palin] has proven that she can electrify the grass roots like few people have in the last 20 years. No matter what she decides to do, there will be a small mother lode of financial support behind her."

Timeline

1964
Born February 11, in Sandpoint, Idaho; three months later family moves to Alaska.

1972
Moves with family to Wasilla, near Anchorage.

1976
Baptized in Little Beaver Lake, becoming "born-again" Christian.

1982
Co-captain of high school basketball team that wins state championship; graduates from Wasilla High School; attends University of Hawaii at Hilo; transfers to Hawaii Pacific University on Oahu.

1983
Attends North Idaho College as a general studies major.

1984
Returns home to work as receptionist; wins "Miss Wasilla" pageant; takes second place and title of "Miss Congeniality" in Miss Alaska pageant.

1985
Attends Matanuski-Susitna College in Palmer, Alaska.

1987
Graduates with journalism degree from University of Idaho; interns for local small-town newspaper.

1988
Lands TV sports reporter job; moves in with sister in Anchorage; elopes with high school sweetheart Todd Palin.

1989
First child, Track, is born; returns to work as TV sportscaster.

1990
Gives birth to second child, Bristol; quits work to stay home.

1992
Elected to Wasilla City Council.

1994
Gives birth to third child, Willow; wins reelection to second council term.

1996

Elected mayor of Wasilla, a post she holds through 2002.

2001

Daughter Piper is born.

2002

Loses bid to become lieutenant governor of Alaska.

2003

Appointed head of Alaska's Oil and Gas Conservation Commission.

2006

Sworn in as governor of Alaska, becoming the first woman and youngest person to hold the office.

2008

Gives birth to fifth child, Trig; chosen by Senator John McCain as his vice-presidential running mate in the 2008 election, becoming the first woman named to a spot on the Republican national ticket; loses the 2008 presidential race to Democrats Barack Obama and Joe Biden.

2009

Resigns as Alaska's governor midway through term; publishes memoir *Going Rogue: An American Life*; remains popular with conservatives and regarded as a possible 2012 contender for the presidency.

Palin and her family on stage at the Republican National Convention in Minneapolis-St. Paul, Minnesota, September 3, 2008.

Sources

Chapter One: Modern Frontier Girl

p. 13,   "Dad never stopped . . ." Kaylene Johnson, *Sarah: How a Hockey Mom Turned the Political Establishment Upside Down* (Carol Stream, Ill.: Tyndall House, 2008), 16.

p. 13-14, "The rest of the kids . . ." Johnson, *Sarah: How a Hockey Mom Turned the Political Establishment Upside Down*, Ibid., 22.

p. 14,   "She was a tough . . ." Lorenzo Benet, *Trailblazer: An Intimate Biography of Sarah Palin* (New York: Simon and Schuster, 2009), 13.

Chapter Two: Miss Congeniality

p. 22,   "I could tell it was . . ." Benet, *Trailblazer: An Intimate Biography of Sarah Palin*, 28.

p. 23,   "He was the best . . ." Ibid., 37.

p. 25,   "I know this sounds hokey . . ." Ibid., 38.

Chapter Four: Learning the Political Game

p. 41,   "Mayor Stein and Nick . . ." Johnson, *Sarah: How a Hockey Mom Turned the Political Establishment Upside Down*, 73.

p. 43,   "John would have . . ." Benet, *Trailblazer: An Intimate Biography of Sarah Palin*, 75.

p. 45,   "She ran on issues . . ." Ibid., 81.

p. 47,   "I want to be president," Jo Becker, Peter S. Goodman, and Michael Powell, "Once Elected, Palin Hired Friends and Lashed Foes," *New York Times*, September 13, 2008.

Chapter 5: Hardball

p. 49,   "Wasilla is moving forward . . ." Johnson, *Sarah: How a Hockey Mom Turned the Political Establishment Upside Down*, 47.

p. 49,   "Because the free exchange . . ." Paul Stuart, "Palin: Library Censorship Inquiries 'Rhetorical'," *Mat-Su Valley Frontiersman*, December 18, 1996.

p. 50,   "This is different . . ." Ibid.

p. 51,   "I didn't get into government . . ." Don Hunter, "McCain picks Alaska Gov. Palin for VP," *Anchorage Daily News*, August 29, 2008.

p. 53,   "We used to have good . . ." Benet, *Trailblazer: An Intimate Biography of Sarah Palin*, 103.

p. 57,   "We would never bill the victim . . ." Jo C. Goode, "Knowles signs sexual assault bill," *Mat-Su Valley Frontiersman*, May 23, 2000.

Chapter 6: Big Time

p. 62,   "She is bright . . ." Jo Becker, Peter Goodman, and Michael Powell, "Once Elected, Palin Hired Friends and Lashed Foes."

p. 69,   "Palin is a master . . ." Andrew Halcro, "What It's Like to Debate Sarah Palin," *Christian Science Monitor*, October 1, 2008.

p. 69,   "Andrew, I watch you . . ." Ibid.

p. 69,   "Anyone who was part . . ." Johnson, *Sarah: How a Hockey Mom Turned the Political Establishment Upside Down*, 97.

p. 70,   "I am a proponent of teaching. . . ." Kyle Hopkins, "Curveballs," October 25, 2006, *AnchorageDaily News*, http://community.adn.com/adnnode/102978.

p. 71,   "She was bold and tough . . ." Johnson, *Sarah: How a Hockey Mom Turned the Political Establishment Upside Down*, 139.

Chapter 7: Governor Sarah

p. 72, "America is looking . . ." Johnson, *Sarah: How a Hockey Mom Turned the Political Establishment Upside Down*, 139.

p. 76, "That bridge to nowhere . . ." Sarah Palin, "Palin's Speech at the Republican National Convention," *New York Times*, September 3, 2008, http://elections.nytimes.com/2008/president/convent ions/videos/20080903_PALIN_SPEECH.html.

p. 77, "To any critics who say . . ." Wesley Loy, "Secret's Out: Palin Pregnant," *Anchorage Daily News*, March 6, 2008.

p. 78, "This new person in your . . ." Benet, *Trailblazer: An Intimate Biography of Sarah Palin,* 188.

p. 78, "Trig's creator, Your . . ." Ibid.

Chapter 8: Her Own Way

p. 87, "It's with great pride and . . ." William Douglas, "McCain's Choice of Palin as Running Mate Draws Mixed Reaction," McClatchy News, August 29, 2008, http://www.mcclatchydc.com/election2008/story/51102.html.

p. 88, "Hillary left 18 million cracks . . ." Michael Cooper and Elizabeth Bumiller, "Alaskan Is McCain's Choice; First Woman on GOP Ticket," *New York Times*, August 29, 2008.

p. 91, "She doesn't have any foreign . . ." Joseph Morton, "Hagel Doubts Palin's Ready,"*Omaha World-Herald*, September 18, 2008.

p. 92, "It's about making life more . . ." Gloria Steinem," "Palin: Wrong Woman, Wrong Message," *Los Angeles Times*, Opinion section, September 4, 2008.

p. 92, "She's not prepared to be . . ." Sean Cockerham and Wesley Loy, "Choice Stuns State Politicians," *Anchorage Daily News*, August 29, 2008, http://www.adn.com/news/politics/story/510249.html.

p. 93, "Can I call you . . ." "Transcript: the Vice Presidential Debate, *New York Times*, October 2, 2008, http://elections.nytimes.com/2008/president/debates/transcripts/vice-presidential-debate.html.

p. 94-95, "I'm sure I'm not the only . . ." Rich Lowry, "The Corner: Projecting Through the Screen," *National Review Online*, October 3, 2008, http://corner.nationalreviewcompost/?q=NDY zMGFiNjQ0MWRjNmI0ZTlkYjg wZTExMjA3MWNiZTk.

p. 96, "The heels are on, the gloves..." Dana Milbank, "Unleashed, Palin Makes a Pit Bull Look Tame," *Washington Post*, October 7, 2008, http://www.washingtonpost.com/wp-dyn/content/article/2008/10/06/AR2008100602935.html.

p. 98, "Okay, listen up . . ." Lyn Sweet, "John McCain on NBC's 'Saturday Night Live.' Tina Fey as Sarah Palin; Ben Affleck hosts," *Chicago Sun Times*, November 2, 2008, http://blogs.suntimes.com/sweet/2008/11/john_mccain_on_nbcs_saturday_n.html.

p. 98, "His success alone commands my respect . . ." John McCain, "John McCain's Concession Speech," November 4, 2008, http://elections.nytimes.com/2008/results/president/speeches/mccain-concession-speech.html.

p. 98, "An impressive new voice in our party. . ." Ibid.

p. 99, "Don't let me miss the open door . . ." Dennis Zaki, "Despite Landslide Defeat, Palin Considers 2012," *Alaskareport.com*, November 10, 2008.

p. 99, "I love my job . . ." Sarah Palin, "Sarah Palin's Resignation Speech," July 3, 2009, Sarah-Palin.com, http://www.sarah-palin.com/2009/07/27/sarah-palinsfarewell-speech/.

p. 100, "Her appeal to people . . ." Todd Purdum, "It Came From Wasilla," *Vanity Fair*, August 2008.

p. 101, "Conservatives have been . . ." Kate Zernike and Monica Davey, "Win or Lose, Many See Palin as Future of Party," *New York Times*, October 29, 2008.

Bibliography

Becker, Jo, Peter S. Goodman, and Michael Powell. "Once Elected, Palin Hired Friends and Lashed Foes." *New York Times*, September 14, 2008.

Benet, Lorenzo. *Trailblazer: An Intimate Biography of Sarah Palin*. New York: Simon and Schuster, 2009.

Carlton, Jim. "Profile of Alaska's Sarah Palin: Governor, Reformer, Mother." *Wall Street Journal*, September 24, 2008.

Gourevitch, Philip. "Letter from Alaska: The State of Sarah Palin." *New Yorker,* September 22, 2008.

Halcro, Andrew. "What it's like to debate Sarah Palin." *Christian Science Monitor,* October 1, 2008, http://www.csmonitor.com/2008/1001/p09s01-coop.html.

Healy, Patrick. "Cordial but Pointed, Palin and Biden Face Off." *New York Times*, October 3, 2008.

Hilley, Joe. *Sarah Palin: A New Kind of Leader*. Grand Rapids, Mich.: Zondervan, 2008.

Johnson, Haynes, and Dan Balz. *The Battle for America 2008: The Story of an Extraordinary Election*. New York: Viking Adult, 2009.

Johnson, Kaylene. *Sarah: How a Hockey Mom Turned the Political Establishment Upside Down*. Carol Stream, Ill.: Tyndall House, 2008.

Katz, Sue. *Thanks But No Thanks*. Arlington, Mass.: Harvard Perspective Press, 2008.

Noah, Timothy. "Sarah Palin's College Daze." Slate.com, October 1, 2008.

Purdum, Todd. "It Came to Wasilla." *Vanity Fair,* August 2009.

Scheiber, Noam. "Barracuda: The resentments of Sarah Palin." *New Republic*, October 22, 2008.

Zernike, Kate. "Palin Joined Alaskan Third Party, Just Not Sarah Palin." *New York Times,* September 3, 2008.

Web Sites

http://www.ontheissues.org/Sarah_Palin.htm
Sarah Palin's views—unfiltered and in her own words—on abortion, education, free trade, the environment, foreign policy, corporations, civil rights, gun control, homeland security, and much more are featured on this Web site.

http://www.facebook.com/sarahpalin
For news and photos of Palin, her Facebook site is a starting point.

http://www.adn.com/sarah-palin
For the most up-to-date coverage of Sarah Palin, visit the Web site of the *Anchorage Daily News.* Through photos, videos, and articles, the Alaska daily traces the life of Palin, from Wasilla High School standout and Republican Party vice presidential candidate to bestselling author.

Photo Credits

2: AP Photo/Al Grillo
8-9: Alamy/Warwick Sloss
10: AP Photo/Charlie Neibergall
11: AP Photo/Heath Family
13: AP Photo/Heath Family
14-15: Wikipedia
16-17: AP Photo/Heath Family
18-19: AP Photo/Heath Family
20: Anchorage Daily News/MCT/Landov
22: AP Photo/Heath Family
25: Anchorage Daily News/MCT/Landov
28: Anchorage Daily News/MCT/Landov
29: Anchorage Daily News/MCT/Landov
31: Alamy/ Ron Niebrugge
34-35: Anchorage Daily News/MCT/Landov
37: AP Photo/Al Grillo
38-39: AP Photo/Al Grillo
44-45: Greg Hensel/Alamy
48: AP Photo/Al Grillo
51: Anchorage Daily News/MCT/Landov
53: Alamy/Warwick Sloss
55: AP Photo
56: Shutterstock
59: Paul Thompson Images/Alamy
60: AP Photo/Al Grillo
64-65: Alamy/ Paul Andrew Lawrence
66: Paul Thompson Images/Alamy
67: AP Photo/Michael Dinneen
71: AP Photo/Al Grillo
72: AP Photo/Chris Miller
74-75: Ron Niebrugge/Alamy
77: Anchorage Daily News/MCT/Landov
80: AP Photo/Al Grillo
82: AP Photo/Kiichiro Sato
84-85: AP Photo/Kiichiro Sato
88-89: BILL Greenblatt/UPI/Landov
94-95: Reuters/Rick Wilking/Landov
102-103: AP Photo/Stephan Savoia

Book cover and interior design by Derrick Carroll of DC Designs.

Index